KEEPING A PONY

KEEPING A PONY

LUCY REES

Stanley Paul

LONDON · SYDNEY · AUCKLAND · JOHANNESBURG

For Jo, with love

Stanley Paul and Co. Ltd

An imprint of Century Hutchinson Ltd
Brookmount House, 62–65 Chandos Place
Covent Garden, London WC2N 4NW

Century Hutchinson Australia (Pty) Ltd
88–91 Albion Street, Surry Hills, NSW 2010

Century Hutchinson New Zealand Ltd
191 Archers Road, PO Box 40-086, Glenfield,
Auckland 10

Century Hutchinson South Africa (Pty) Ltd
PO Box 337, Bergvlei 2012, South Africa

First published 1989

Set in Linotron 202 Souvenir by Rowland Phototypesetting Ltd,
Bury St Edmunds, Suffolk

Printed and bound in Great Britain by
Butler & Tanner Ltd, Frome and London

British Library Cataloguing in Publication Data

Rees, Lucy, 1943–
   Keeping a pony.
   1. Livestock: Ponies. Care—Manuals
   I. Title
   636.1'6

ISBN 0 09 171490 7

Contents

Contents

Photograph Acknowledgements

Photographs of a pony trotting (page 29), Peruvian *paso fino* ponies (page 29), a hunter clip (page 129), plaiting a tail and a plaited tail (page 191), and the Pony Club mounted games (page 194) are by Bob Langrish.

An American pacer (page 30), New Zealand rug (page 73), ploughing harness (page 97), and a trace clip (page 130) are by Kit Houghton.

The photograph of Princess Elizabeth and King George VI on page 90 is by kind permission of *Riding Magazine*.

All others are by Lucy Rees.

1 Beginnings

Some fifty million years ago, when London was a crocodile-infested swamp and giant mammals roamed the earth, the ancestors of what were to become ponies were small dog-like creatures that ran on three-toed hoofs. They lived in North America, which was not where it is now. Scampering up the trees they wandered through were little squirrel-like animals that might have been the ancestors of the apes that were our ancestors.

Times change. Animals migrate, climates change, new horizons open and continents drift. Hunted by sabre-tooth tigers, those pre-ponies got faster, running on one toe. They grew longer legs, longer noses and bigger brains. But on another continent the greatest explosion in brain size of all time was happening, and by the time shaggy, primitive ponies had evolved, ape-men were gradually struggling upright. Nobody quite knows when they first met; it might have been in eastern Asia, the lights of the first cave fires scaring off the wild-eyed, inquisitive herds.

For thousands of years now people have been involved with horses, hunting and eating them, painting them, taming them, breaking them to haul and carry and be ridden. They have worshipped and sacrificed them, beaten them, played games and won wars with them, and trained them in a hundred different ways. It is an association so ancient it seems natural. If you have just decided to join in, welcome.

As times have changed, so have ideas and knowledge. We are probably more humane towards horses than ever before, but so we should be since we use them solely for our pleasure. At first there seems a lot to know and as a novice once put it, 'everyone

9

who's ever been within smelling distance of a horse is an expert.'

Take heart. Good sound common sense is often a better guide than high-flown ideas. But even with the best will in the world it is possible to neglect or mistreat a pony without meaning to, and this is where this book comes in. It is intended as a guide not just for the first-time pony owner but for anyone who wants to understand the basics, the whys and wherefores, of keeping a pony. Too often we are told to do this or that without being told the reasons, which leads to confusion and blind rule following. If you want to develop good horse sense, listen by all means, but ask why too. Often you will find that the experts have different aims, so their methods differ. Search for knowledge based on understanding rather than on rules, and you will have a firm foundation for keeping your pony healthy and happy, using him well, and opening up a whole new world for yourself.

2 The Horse's Body

The results of the horse's evolution produced an animal superbly fitted for life on the open plain or among forests, hills and mountains in temperate regions. The origin of the modern horse is not clear, but one theory says that there are four main types. Two probably arose in desert regions, for they are better at resisting heat and lack of water. Lightly built, they have hard, dense bone, sparse mane and tail, and are long-legged. The smaller of these is thought to be the ancestor of the modern Arab, which in turn gave rise to other speedy 'hot-blooded' breeds. The taller, whose nearest modern relative may be the Akhal-Teke, is not seen in western Europe. Both the other two types are found amongst British native ponies. They are more resistant to cold and wet, fattening up well on poor feed, with thicker, less dense bone and feet, and thick mane and tail. The bigger of these two, the typical 'cold-blood' pony, resulted in the solid Highland and Iceland type: the smaller, lighter type, the so-called Celtic pony, is seen in its most unchanged form in the Exmoor.

Over the centuries careful breeding from these original types has produced extremes: the massive docile Shire, slow-tempered, straight-shouldered, and capable of pulling great weights; the tall, hot-blooded Thoroughbred, fastest of all horses; hard-working Shetlands; and toy Falabellas. Despite this variety, horses and ponies are much more uniform in appearance than dogs. The only major difference between them is that Arabs have one vertebra less in the chest region, and hence one rib less than other breeds.

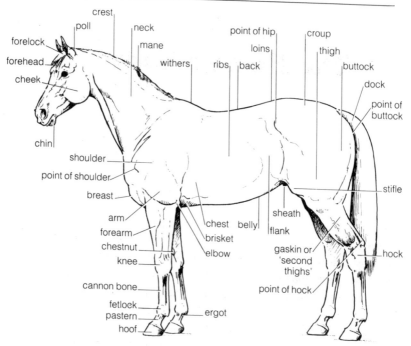

Figure 1 *The points of the horse*

Basic Anatomy

Like most grazers, the horse has long jaws and hence a long head, which means he can see over the top of grass while eating. The furry muzzle, seen best on cold-blooded types in winter, enables him to break ice and eat through snow, unlike the bald-muzzled cow. Native ponies often grow moustaches too. The whiskers are an important sense organ and should not be cut off.

Different breeds have different-shaped noses, the extremes being the dish-faced Arab and the Roman-nosed draught horse. The big nose of the cold-bloods is thought to help in warming cold air before it reaches the lungs. The nose contains two organs of smell: the ordinary nasal organ and the Jacobson's organ, which is a blind pouch deep in the nose. It can only be used if the horse takes a deep breath and forces air into it by rolling his upper lip back over his

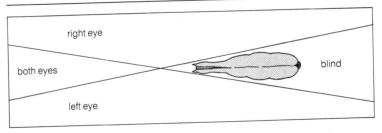

right eye

both eyes

left eye

blind

Figure 2 How a horse sees. He cannot see behind him, nor immediately in front, but further in front he can see with both eyes so he can judge distance

nostrils (flehmen). This is seen especially when a stallion smells a mare or when a horse tastes something unfamiliar.

The eyes are set on the side of the head, allowing the horse to see almost all round himself. Standing straight, he cannot see immediately in front of his nose or behind him; nor can he see his body, his rider or his own feet. If a horse is tied up short, sudden movements behind him may startle him into kicking since he cannot see what is making the movement. A sudden grab at his foot may surprise and alarm him; he may also tread blindly on your foot.

Welsh mountain pony unable to see a carrot in front of his nose, for it comes in his blind zone. Note the whip held correctly with the loop round Lowri's wrist

13

The eyes are more sensitive to movement, especially in the distance, than ours. They do not focus like ours: a horse must move her head up, down or sideways to focus. Only when her head is low can she see the ground in front of her feet or behind her heels clearly. To see something on the ground beside her feet she has to tilt her head sideways or even skip sideways (shying). It is difficult for a beginner to know what a horse is looking at, but by remembering these differences you can watch and learn. Many mistakes in handling a pony can be avoided by making allowance for these differences in ways of seeing and by giving the horse the freedom to swing her head about so she can see properly.

The ears are fur-lined to prevent dust, seeds and insects getting in. Do not shave this fur off. The ears can be pointed in any direction that interests the pony or flattened in case of fighting. A horse with his ears back is not necessarily bad-tempered, merely concentrating on what is behind him. However, this may mean he is uneasy and would like to be sure he can back out of trouble.

The neck is long and flexible. It acts as a counterbalance when the horse is moving, and its freedom is important when the horse is making great efforts, as in jumping. There are seven bones in the neck. The second of these, the axis, swivels on a peg in the canal where the spinal cord passes down the middle of the backbone. A bang on the head can jerk this peg and break the spinal cord, causing death. Long-lasting injury can result from a lesser blow since the spinal cord is not protected from above at this point.

A strong ligament runs the whole length of the spine, linking the backbone through its upper surfaces. When it is contracted the back shortens and the head and tail are raised. This is seen especially when the horse is alarmed or is getting ready for action.

The bony knobs along the horse's back are not the vertebrae themselves but the spines sticking out from their upper surfaces. A well-fitting saddle makes sure that weight is not placed on the flesh immediately above these spines, which would cause bruising, but on the muscle on each side. A badly fitting saddle causes sores and abscesses, especially if it presses on the withers where the skin runs directly over the dorsal spines. There are usually six bones in the loin region and this part of the spine is not fit to carry weight: indeed, many ponies object to weight behind the saddle. The spine continues behind the hips and down into the tail as the dock.

There are usually eighteen ribs (sometimes nineteen, but Arabs have seventeen).

The horse's shoulder as we see it is the shoulderblade; there is no collarbone. The upper-arm bone is part of the body but sticks out at the elbow. The upper part of a horse's front leg corresponds to our forearm, his knee to our wrist. The knee is therefore a complicated joint with numerous small bones.

The cannon bone corresponds to the middle bone in our hand, greatly strengthened. The bones corresponding to the first and fifth hand bones have completely disappeared. The second and fourth bones are small; they start at the knee but taper to nothing halfway down the cannon bone. They fuse with the cannon bone when the horse is about four years old. If a horse is worked too young the loose ends rub against the cannon bone, causing a bony growth known as a splint. This is painful while it is developing but gives no trouble once set.

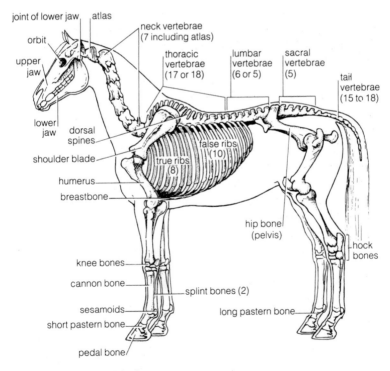

Figure 3 Skeleton of the horse

Only the middle 'finger' remains as the pastern. At the top of it, in the fetlock joint, is a small extra bone, the sesamoid. The end of the 'finger' continues in the foot, the hoof corresponding to our nail. The chestnut, a strange horny growth on the inside of the upper foreleg and lower hindleg, may also be a nail. So may ergots, which are found in the hair on the back of the fetlock.

In the back leg too the upper bone is part of the body, the stifle joint corresponding to our knee. Like us, a horse can slip a kneecap (patella). The hock, our ankle, is strong. The rest of the leg is as the front leg except that the reduced bones do not form splints.

The skin varies in thickness and sensitivity over the body: the areas behind the elbow and between the back legs are the thinnest, but those on the flanks and belly usually the most irritable. It can be twitched and wriggled to remove flies, but if a pony wriggles it irritably when you stroke him it may mean he is sore there.

The coat is short in summer and long in winter. Old ponies keep their winter coats longer, and regrow them earlier, than younger ones. Native ponies grow good thick winter coats, but those of Arab or Thoroughbred blood suffer more from cold and wet in winter. Their finer skin also makes them more prone to rain and mud rash.

The Teeth

Generally forty teeth in males and thirty-six in mares, for mares usually lack tushes or canine teeth. Unlike cows and sheep, ponies have the same number of teeth in upper and lower jaws. From the centre front working backwards on one side, there are first three incisors (cutting teeth), then maybe one tush in the middle of a

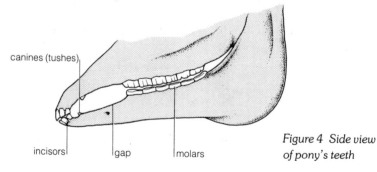

canines (tushes)

incisors   gap   molars

Figure 4 Side view of pony's teeth

toothless gap, and six back teeth or molars (grinding teeth) hidden in the cheek. There may also be one wolf tooth, a small tooth just in front of the row of molars.

The bars are the toothless stretches of gum between the front and back teeth. A snaffle bit acts on the bars rather than on the corners of the mouth. The bars may become bruised and finally insensitive (hard mouth) if the bit is abused by heavy hands.

Ponies, like us, grow two sets of teeth. The first or milk teeth have almost no root. They are replaced by permanent teeth with long roots. Unlike ours, these teeth keep growing throughout the pony's life until they wear out in extreme old age. They change in ways that make it possible to tell his age.

Learning to age a pony from his teeth takes experience which can only be won by examining the mouth of every pony whose age is definitely known – usually only the pedigree ones. As you get better at it you may be surprised to discover how many people have been misled about their pony's age when buying. However, the wear on the teeth does depend on how the pony has been fed, so in older ponies ageing is uncertain.

Changes in the front teeth
By the age of one a pony has cut all his milk teeth. At two and a half to three, that is, in the winter or spring before he is three, he loses his central incisors (middle two teeth, top and bottom) and replaces them with permanent teeth, much as a child of about five does. As with children, the milk teeth are small and white, the permanent ones bigger and yellower, so the difference is easily seen. When these teeth change the pony cannot crop grass; he may lose weight suddenly, become very bad-tempered, have swollen gums or palate, and may eat earth or develop other unusual habits like playing with water to cool his mouth.

At three and a half to four the second (lateral) pairs of milk teeth are replaced.

At four and a half to five the third (corner) pairs are replaced but the permanent ones do not grow to their full height. By six the corner incisors are fully risen and the top surface has begun to wear. By seven the top corner incisor overhangs the bottom one so that it forms a little hook at the back. By eight this hook has disappeared again.

17

Figure 5a Teeth at 3 years   Figure 5b Teeth at 4 years

Figure 5c Teeth at 5 years   Figure 5d Teeth at 6 years

Figure 5e Teeth at 7 years   Figure 5f Teeth at 8 years

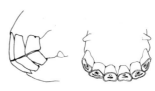

Figure 5g Teeth at 9 years   Figure 5h Teeth at 10 years

Galvayne's groove

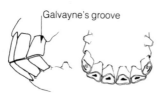

Figure 5i Teeth at 13 years   Figure 5j Teeth at 17 years

Figure 5k Teeth at 20–25 years

The central black mark on the surface of the tooth is now smaller and more rounded than in a six-year-old and has no dent in it. The surface is now more triangular than oval.

From eight onwards it becomes difficult to tell the age reliably, which is why in sales you seldom come across a horse advertised as more than eight. He may however be called 'aged'. This does not necessarily mean 'ancient', merely that he is more than eight, the judgement being left to the buyer.

At nine the surface of the tooth is more triangular and there are now definitely two black marks, one behind the other.

At ten the angle of the teeth is more pronounced.

At eleven a groove (Galvayne's groove) appears in the top of the top corner incisor. You can feel it by running your thumbnail over the tooth. During the next ten or so years it grows downwards; by the age of fifteen it comes halfway down and by nineteen it runs from top to bottom. It then starts disappearing from the top, so that by about twenty-five only the lower half remains. By about the age of thirty it has disappeared altogether.

During this time the teeth gradually become more sloped and also rounder and longer. They start wearing out altogether at thirty-five or so, but this depends on the amount of wear they have had. Ponies kept on very sandy soil, for instance, often have teeth worn beyond their age. However, for practical purposes, a pony's appearance after the age of about eighteen is as good a guide to how much life is left in him as is his real age.

Canines (tushes)

Male horses grow one stubby tooth (a canine or tush) in the middle of the gap between front and back teeth, top and bottom, when they are about five. In about one in four mares there is a tush in the lower jaw; very few mares have upper ones too.

Back teeth

A young horse has a full set of six milk molars which get replaced by permanent teeth at about the same time as the front teeth. There is also a small premolar, the wolf tooth, just in front of the molars. This normally falls out at about the age of six, but in some cases it does not and can cause trouble (dislike of the bit, head-tossing, boring, rearing) if the bit presses on it and hurts. As a general rule it is better to ride a

19

young horse in a rubber bit to minimize discomfort. If wolf teeth cause trouble they can be removed.

Problems with teeth

If the jaws are not the same length the teeth do not meet in front and do not wear down evenly. A parrot-mouthed pony has a short lower jaw, so the top front teeth overlap the bottom ones. This is a serious genetic fault, for the pony cannot graze properly and will need his teeth filing regularly.

Often the molars do not meet exactly either, so that as they grow the unworn parts turn into spikes. These hang off the inside edge of the lower teeth and on the outside edge of the upper ones, causing the pony to drop her food and even tear her cheek or tongue. Any pony that appears to have difficulty eating, or is sloppy about it, should have her teeth checked and rasped.

Checking the back teeth

Put your hand in the pony's mouth from the side and take a firm hold of the whole tongue in your fist. Pull it gently to one side out of his mouth. This prevents him biting since he will not bite his own tongue. Now slide the fingers of your other hand carefully along the inside of his cheek to feel whether the outer sides of the top back teeth are sharp. Take care! The spurs can be very sharp, and if your fingers stray between his teeth he can still bite. Horses have powerful jaws. If you think the teeth need rasping call the vet. Some farriers also rasp teeth. If the teeth need doing regularly or if your pony hates vets, you can ask to be taught to do it yourself.

The Digestive System

The horse has a simple stomach and cannot vomit or regurgitate food. Unlike dogs, which vomit easily, horses are choosy about their food and suffer severe pain from colic if bad food is eaten. The stomach is small compared to the size of the animal, and in a natural life a horse tends to keep it half full, rather than filling it up at meals and fasting in between. Hence the golden rule of feeding 'little and often'.

From the stomach, half-digested food goes to the small intestine, a muscular tube 10–20 feet long, where it is broken down further and absorbed. However, most is passed on to the large intestine. Animals cannot digest the material that plants are mostly made of, so plant-eating animals store bacteria in their guts to break it down for them. In the horse these bacteria are in the large intestine. Antibiotics tend to act against the bacteria so they can upset the digestion somewhat. There is a sharp bend in the large intestine so blockage can occur here if, for example, the horse is suddenly stabled after being out at grass and is fed large quantities of dry food. Impactive colic will then result.

Like his other organ systems, a pony's digestion works better when he can move about freely and live the kind of life he is adapted to.

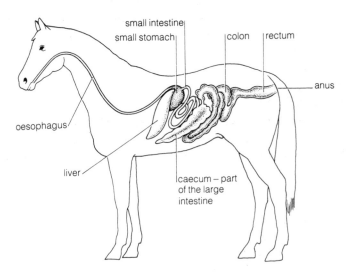

Figure 6 Digestive system

Blood Circulation

The circulation is basically the same as in other mammals, but it is worth noting that it only works properly in the lower legs when the horse can move about freely. Stabled ponies, especially on rich diets, may get filled legs, that is, puffy, fluid-filled legs, like those of heavily pregnant women. When the pony is exercised the circulation improves and carries away this extra fluid.

21

Many ponies have slight irregularities in the heart beat (murmurs) but in most these seem to cause no problem.

Muscles, Tendons and Ligaments

As in other animals, the muscles, especially those of the neck, shoulder and rump, are built up by regular exercise. Muscles attach to bones either directly or through tendons. Some tendons are very long, like those that move the foot: the muscles that contract and pull them are high in the upper leg, so it is easy to strain these tendons.

Ligaments are made of the same stuff as tendons but they attach bones to each other rather than bone to muscle. Ligaments take a long time to mend as the blood supply to them is poor.

Lungs

Ponies have large lungs that, like the circulation and the digestive system, work best when the animal is out in the open air. Ponies get coughs and wheezes easily if they are kept in stuffy, dusty stables.

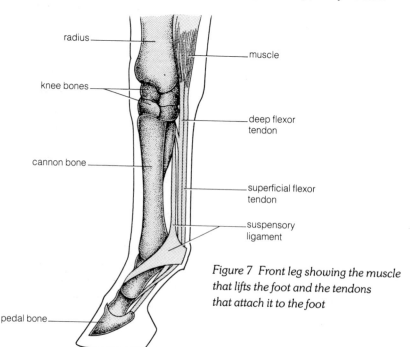

radius

knee bones

cannon bone

pedal bone

muscle

deep flexor tendon

superficial flexor tendon

suspensory ligament

Figure 7 Front leg showing the muscle that lifts the foot and the tendons that attach it to the foot

3 The Psychology of the Horse

Instinctively, any pony reacts just like her ancestors, and will continue to do so unless she has been trained to behave otherwise. If we look at the behaviour of ponies in the wild we can understand our tame ponies much better.

Like all plant-eaters, ponies are good to eat and, in their natural state, must protect themselves against wolves and lions. Having no horns or other form of defence, the horse runs away from danger and threat. Ponies have no inclination to fight or to face unpleasantness: they go away instead. This flightiness is more marked among the hot-blooded types; the cold-blooded ones, perhaps because they evolved in marsh and forest where thoughtless flight might be disastrous, sometimes freeze when frightened and refuse to move, until they explode suddenly into action.

Ponies do not seem to forget that their ancestors were hunted and eaten, and even in twentieth-century Britain they see tigers, or suspect tigers, surprisingly often. Many of their other natural feelings stem from the fact that they are the hunted, not the hunters. Thus they have no natural tendency to attack other animals. They will defend themselves by kicking if they cannot run away, but they do not attack unless they have learned to.

They are friendly, living in groups: there is safety in numbers. No pony would ever choose to live alone, and most are nervous, or quietly miserable, unless they have company. They are interested in meeting other ponies, and become excited by the smell of others nearby. Particular friends are important to ponies, and sometimes two will form such a strong friendship that it is almost impossible to separate them. Ponies extend their friendship to people too, and

23

some ponies even become friends with their ancestral enemies, dogs and cats.

Escaping from unpleasantness and fear is a basic reaction, but no less basic is the reaction of clinging to friends. When startled, a group of ponies bunches together, just as a foal runs to its dam. All but the boldest of horses depend on their friends for support and courage; where there is a confident leader, ponies are great followers. This dependency, one of their strongest characteristics, is shown to people they trust as well.

All animals that live in groups are good at communicating with each other, and ponies are extremely sensitive to one another's signs. They signal to one another by voice, movement and expression, and by changing the body outline. They are quick to notice signs of nervousness: when one pony in a herd becomes alert because it has spotted something suspicious, all the others take note and get ready to run. They are also quick to react to our moods, and nervousness in us makes them want to go away too.

Since their safety depends on their feet, ponies are extremely careful about where they tread. They prefer to follow each other along well-trodden, familiar paths; they dislike hollow-sounding bridges and ramps; they panic if their feet get tangled in wire or caught suddenly; they avoid puddles and rivers if possible; bogs terrify them. They cannot see properly without being able to move their heads freely, so the experience of being haltered and tied is at first doubly frightening.

For an animal who feels his safety depends on being able to escape, being restricted or shut in is a horrifying experience. Even to a horse who is used to it, stabling is a stress, and ponies seldom choose to stay inside when they can be outside, free. Many ponies bred on the moor become frantic if shut in.

Similarly, they feel vulnerable when lying down. They can doze standing up, but to get a good sleep they must lie down, and they will not do so unless they feel safe. Sick horses will often refuse to lie down, probably because they know they cannot get up quickly. In any case, horses do not cope well with long-term pain, unlike cats and dogs: in the wild a sick horse is soon prey to the wolves.

Ponies like to feel they know what is going on, so they are inquisitive and like exploring. They are excellent at learning their way and at finding their way home even in strange territory if they want to,

24

though no one knows how they do it. They are also brilliant at remembering places where surprises, pleasant or unpleasant, have happened. They are particularly aware of changes in familiar places: a newly fallen tree, a freshly painted door or even an unexpected herd of cows interest and excite them, and may arouse their suspicions until they are sure no danger lurks in the new arrangement. On their home ground they have preferred spots for activities such as rolling, sleeping and loafing in certain weather conditions.

Perhaps because they are often bred and raised closer to their natural state, ponies tend to react more instinctively and with more 'horse sense' than bigger horses. They are less unreasonably nervous, but they are more likely to refuse to be driven into situations of genuine danger. When handling or riding a pony, it is always best to realize that he has a particular view of the world in regard to what is dangerous or desirable, and that even when his view conflicts with ours he is not necessarily being silly. A pony may, for instance, suddenly refuse to enter a trailer she 'knows' is safe, and there may be several reasons for this. The trailer may be parked so that the inside is in deep shadow, possibly concealing all manner of tigers; the ramp may sound and feel different from usual; there may be strange flags in the background which signal a different situation to the pony; everybody may be in a state of nervous excitement which makes the pony suspect they know of unrevealed dangers and so on. All these pony reasons are reasonable, though we may be too biased to see them. From a pony's point of view, jumping a jump that can perfectly well be avoided is pretty silly. Respecting a pony's feelings is the first step in understanding how to deal with them.

Any pony's behaviour is a product of not only his nature but also of his past and present handling. Young ponies love exploring and learning but they are intimidated on their own and need a sensible and understanding guide, just as we might if we were suddenly plunged into a strange and alarming new world. As they are treated, so they become. A pony that has been shown and taught things in a sympathetic, encouraging way will be trustful, willing and interested; a pony that has been beaten into going forward when afraid will become stubborn and refuse to consider new experiences sensibly; a pony that has had his feelings ignored by insensitive riders becomes sullen, dull and insensitive himself. A pony's reaction to unpleasantness is to avoid it, and if he has unpleasantness forced upon him he may bite and kick to rid himself of it, or even what he thinks may be the threat of it. All these different behaviours require different behaviour from us; part of the art and fascination of horsemanship is developing the ability to understand and adjust in the search to make the relationship between horse and human as fruitful and pleasant as possible.

4 Movement

On the flat the pony usually moves in one of four forward paces. He can also move backwards, sideways and do various skips, leaps, bucks and indeterminate shuffles, especially over rough ground.

The Paces

The *walk* has four beats and the pony always has at least two feet on the ground. The sequence of footfalls is: right hind, right fore, left hind, left fore, right hind. . . . The beats are not quite evenly spaced.

The *trot* has two beats, the left fore and right hind (left diagonal) hitting the ground together, followed by the right fore and left hind (right diagonal). These two beats are absolutely even. In between there is a short moment of suspension when the pony is in the air.

The *canter* is an asymmetrical pace, that is, unlike the walk and trot, what happens on one side is not mirrored by what happens on the other. Watching a canter, we see that one front leg appears to 'lead' or come farther forward than the other. In fact, this is the last foot to hit the ground before the moment of suspension; each pace really starts from the back. On the left lead the sequence is: right hind, right diagonal (right fore and left hind together), left fore, suspension, giving three beats followed by a gap. If you imagine yourself doing this you will see that if you were leading on the left you would tend to be going to the left, and in fact, if cantering in a circle a pony leads with his inside leg; along a slope he leads with his uphill leg.

At any time in the canter the pony's whole weight is supported only by the foot or feet that have just hit the ground, the others being in the

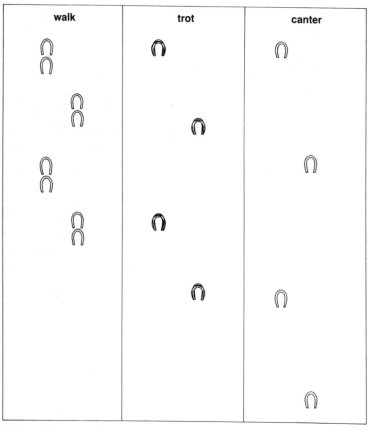

Figure 8 *Footprints at different paces*
At a walk, if the pony is stepping well underneath him (see chapter 21) his footprints overlap more than if he is walking sloppily. This is called 'tracking up'. This pony is walking fairly briskly

air. Since he is going at some speed, cantering or galloping puts far more strain on his legs than trotting.

The *gallop* is similar to the canter, but there are four beats since the hind foot of the diagonal hits the ground before the corresponding forefoot. On the right lead the sequence is: left hind, right hind, left fore, right fore, and a longer period of suspension.

Other paces: at the running walk (slow gait or *paso fino*) the feet go down absolutely regularly one after the other, unlike the walk. The

Pony trotting. He is carrying himself nicely, but the rider would do better to have her lower leg further back so her heel comes under her hip. The pony is wearing exercise bandages in front

Peruvian paso fino *ponies doing a running walk*

American pacer. The two legs on one side both move together. The horse has the lightest of driving harness and a sheepskin noseband, which stops it from tipping its head too high (or it can't see)

rack (*paso largo* or the *tölt* in Iceland ponies) is a much faster version of this; a good racking horse goes faster than a canter. Both these paces are extremely comfortable for the rider, far smoother than the trot or canter.

In pacing (confusingly, there is a distinct pace called pacing) the two legs on one side go down together, followed by the two on the other side. Racing pacers are slightly faster than trotters.

The ability to do these paces is bred for in America, but the horse usually needs some encouragement to develop them. Ambling, a slower version of pacing, is also more comfortable than a trot and was once widely cultivated in Britain.

In backing the sequence of footfalls is the same as in the trot, one diagonal after the other, not as in the walk.

Balance

It is helpful to think of the pony as a seesaw, the middle being about where a rider's knee comes. The front legs tend to carry more weight than the back ones. Watching a pony, you will see that at faster paces the head is carried higher and the hindquarters tend to be lowered. This is because the main power comes from behind: like a rear-wheel-drive car, the pony pushes himself forwards rather than dragging himself forwards with his front legs. As he goes faster he tends to bring his hocks underneath him so that he carries more of his weight on his back legs, using his power more efficiently because he is not wasting it driving his front end down into the ground.

The rider's weight at first upsets the balance, tipping it farther forward ('on the forehand'), but the pony soon learns to rebalance himself. Through schooling the balance is again lifted from the front. A well-trained pony carries more of his weight on his back legs than his front (you can tell by how quickly his front and hind shoes wear out) so that his power is instantly available. However, any pony is unbalanced and made heavy by two riding faults: leaning forward, which most beginners do out of nervousness, and heavy-handedness or keeping a dead hand on the rein. This makes most ponies lean on the bit, failing to rebalance themselves. Unfortunately many riders make the problem worse by pulling the reins harder. The real solution is to make the pony use his back legs more, by use of the leg aids, and to refuse to give him anything to lean on (see chapter 21).

Normally a pony turns by pushing his front end round with his rear. It is possible for the pony to turn his head and neck to the right while the rest of him is making a left turn; if the back legs are pushing him to the left that is the way he will go. In fact, unridden horses often turn in this way. In Western riding this is recognized, but in English riding great stress is placed on the idea that the pony should lead with his head, with the unfortunate result that most novice riders think that they should pull him round by using the rein. If this is coupled with heaviness in front from the seesaw effect described above, the result is unpleasant for both pony and rider, being little more than a wrestling match. Since the pony himself turns from the rear, it is far more effective as well as kinder to push the hindquarters in the desired direction, making a slight adjustment to the head position only if wanted.

31

A country ride. The front rider is a novice: she wears unsuitable high-heeled boots and her toe is lower than her heel so her lower leg is tight. Like most beginners, she has her stirrups too short and her leg so far forward that she could not stand in them without leaning right forward. Her back is slumped and stiff, her shoulder hunched and her hand dead. All this encourages the pony to be heavy on the forehand and the saddle to slip forwards.

The second rider has a far better seat. His shoulder, hip and heel make one straight vertical line so he is well balanced. His back is stretched and free, his hand light but his leg firm. An active rider rather than a passenger, he affects the way his pony moves: she brings her hindleg further under her than the first horse, and carries her head higher and more gracefully.

Both ponies look fit but underweight, as is typical of many trekking ponies working hard in August

A pony will not move freely unless he can see properly, knows where he is going, or has great faith in the rider. The faster he moves the less he can see, and the higher his head the less he can see of his feet. Where the footing is difficult, then, he will probably want to go slowly, stopping from time to time to put his head down and work out the next series of steps. If the rider prevents him from looking properly by keeping the reins tight, he may refuse to go forward. In unknown places he may be unwilling to canter since the canter, being an uneven pace, is less stable than the trot. A timid or young pony is often not bold enough to go forward in a strange place alone and may want to stop every few yards, neck stuck up in the air, to make sure the way ahead is safe. If pushed unsympathetically before he is sure of his ground, he may well start going backwards instead of forwards.

Action

Different breeds have typically different styles of movement. Most cobby types are steady movers but tend to be heavy on the forehand unless well ridden. The true Welsh breeds (sections A, C and D, see page 47) pick their feet up very high; Welsh cobs are tremendous trotters though relatively less exciting at a canter. Arabs are springy, with a floating action that comes from long periods of suspension; a less easy action for the novice rider but a delicious sensation for the experienced. Thoroughbreds and show-pony types tend to extend the shoulder well forward with a lower, 'daisy-cutting' action: comfortable but not dramatic to watch.

5 An Eye for a Horse

Being able to tell how good a pony is, how it will move and how it will stand up to a lifetime's work, is part of horsemanship. Developing a critical eye for what is known as conformation is part of the expert's art.

Conformation, the physical shape and balance of the animal, is a combination of desirable and undesirable points. Different breeds have been developed for different purposes, so what is important in one type is not necessarily so in another. However, if you understand how conformation affects function you can adapt your eye to your need.

The condition of the pony does not affect its genetic conformation, although a pony that has always been underfed will end up with poorer conformation than one that has been well fed. However, it is important to be able to separate condition from conformation. Most novices are more impressed by a well-fed horse of poor conformation than by a thin one of better quality. You can learn the differences better at a sale, where horses and ponies of every type, age and condition rub shoulders, than at a show where generally only well-fed quality animals are seen.

When judging a pony, first have a good look at him from a distance. The overall effect should be harmonious and pleasing: the shoulder should balance the hindquarter, the length balance the height. The legs should be straight, and as you walk round the pony, he should be standing square on them like a table. The leg joints are designed to work in a column with weight placed on them from above; any crookedness results in strain on the joints when the animal is worked.

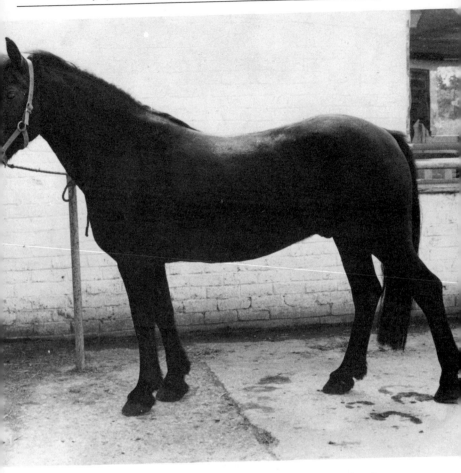

Cobby pony about 14 hands. This pony has a bright, kind eye, nice head and neck for his type, and strong hindquarters and legs. He is, however, very long in the back. He will be a steady mover, comfortable to ride and easy to keep: a good choice for a novice large child or small adult although an experienced rider might find him a little heavy.

His headcollar is too far down his nose: if he pulled suddenly it could damage his nose. His head markings are a star and stripe. He should have more feather but it has been trimmed, purely out of prejudice

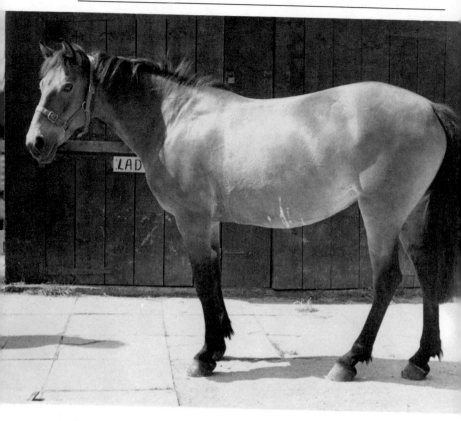

Crossbred dun pony about 13.1 hands will be uncomfortable to ride and heavy in hand, for her hindquarters are higher than her withers, her shoulder is straight and her neck short although well-shaped. She also looks over at the knee, while the white mark on her right inside coronet shows that she brushes behind. However she has a charming, kind face and looks like an easy keeper. She is in very good condition, fit and shining.

Her headcollar is of the type that can be removed after a bridle is put on top, but it is too tight round her nose

Shetland cross. This strong pony is so badly put together that he seems to be a scrap-heap of unwanted parts. His head and neck fit a pony two hands bigger. His shoulder is very straight and his hindquarters weak. However, in a tiny child's pony character is really more important than conformation but unfortunately he looks grumpy too. He is so strong that if he misbehaved a child would have no chance of controlling him. He would, though, live on very little keep

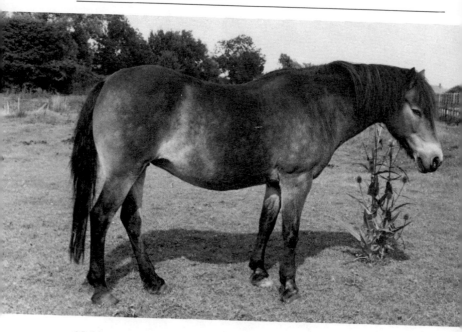

12.2 hand pony showing the typical Exmoor coloration, with a mealy nose, toad eyes and yellow shading underneath. Good neck and withers and a short strong back, but his straight shoulder and short straight pasterns would give a short, jarring stride

The shape of the head relates less to function than do other points of conformation, but most horsemen are strongly biased in favour of a smallish head, with a straight or slightly dished nose, as broad a forehead as possible and a small muzzle. Extremely dish-faced ponies have Arab blood; in the Welsh breeds and the Dartmoor slight dishing accompanies the great breadth of forehead that shows intelligence. Most large cold-blooded ponies have straighter profiles. A coarse, 'jug' head is always considered undesirable, together with the small pig eyes that often go with it. Both are thought to show stupidity, though their owners might more fairly be described as strong-minded and unimaginative, but reliable and hardworking.

The teeth should meet in an even line: a parrot mouth or undershot lower jaw is most undesirable as the pony cannot graze properly.

A big, bold, lustrous eye is desirable, as are small alert ears. A pony that rolls its eyes may be nervous and bad-tempered in character, but some bold ponies naturally show white round the eye without being temperamental.

There should be a good width between the bones of the jowl at the throat (test with your fist), so the air passage is not restricted. In a riding pony the neck should be long ('a good length of rein') and narrow where it joins the head. A short thick neck is very powerful and tends to give a heavy feel on the rein, but it enables a working pony to develop more power against the collar. The top of the neck should be a graceful curve; the under line should also be curved upwards. A downward curve in either part (ewe neck) is a distinct fault as the pony sticks her nose out and up and cannot give to the rein. In a stallion the neck has a distinct crest and is heavier (the forehead is also broader, the cheeks jowlier and the musculature heavier).

Good withers are slightly raised above the level of the base of the neck and the back. The rounded, 'mutton' withers common in small ponies do not hold a saddle well. Withers that are high or knife-like also give problems with a saddle, though this fault is less common in ponies.

The slope of the shoulder, from the point of the shoulder to the withers, profoundly affects the way a pony moves. The more upright the shoulder, the less the foreleg is extended; this type of shoulder (which often goes with a short strong neck on cobby types) is more suited to a collar and farmwork. The pony moves with a short choppy gait. In a riding pony the shoulder should be sloping to give a longer, freer stride. In Thoroughbreds and the show-type riding ponies derived from them, the generous, sloping shoulder combines with a well-sloped humerus (upper-arm bone) to give great extension, especially at the walk and gallop. The trot is long and low.

A well-laid-back shoulder combined with a more upright humerus is seen in the Welsh types and to an extreme in the Hackney. The combination gives an upright stance and the freedom to lift the foreleg in the high action so typical of these breeds. Other moorland breeds tend to show the same combination to a less marked degree: the high-stepping, sure-footed action is desirable in a pony that moves over rough ground. In Arab types the shoulder tends to be more upright but the shortness of gait this implies is offset by the shorter back and powerful hindquarters, which give great forward thrust.

39

The forearm should be straight, the knee large, bony and flat when seen from the front. Small, round or podgy knees are not good. The many bones in the knee joint work more efficiently if they are large and well set. The cannon bone carries all the animal's weight and should be short and stout. It should continue the line of the forearm when seen both from the front and from the side. Any hint that it does not (over at the knee, back at the knee, bow-legged, knock-kneed) is a distinct fault as the weight is thrown unevenly on the joints above and below. Cobby types tend to have more 'bone' (measured round the cannon bone just below the knee) than Arab or Thoroughbred types; however, the cob bone is less solid. In any type, though, the more bone the stronger the leg.

The fetlock joint should be round. The pastern below it also has a great effect on action. A short, upright pastern gives a jarring step; too sloping a pastern breaks down with hard work, as does too long a pastern if it is weak. The ideal, a long, strong pastern sloping at about 50° in front, gives great spring and is typically one of the Arab's strongest points, enabling him to show the characteristic floating action.

The forefoot should be round, its angle continuing that of the pastern, and should point neither in nor out (pigeon-toed, splay-footed). From underneath the heels should be open, the frog generous and the sole dished, not flat, though some foot faults can be altered by a skilful farrier.

The chest cavity contains the heart and lungs, so it should be both deep and wide. A pony with 'both legs coming out of the same hole' is weedy and tends to be a bad doer. A very wide chest, as in some of the heavier working ponies, leads to a rolling, lumbering canter and almost no gallop. A small child is better mounted on a narrow pony, or her legs have little effect. Small boys find broadness especially uncomfortable, for the set of their hips is different from girls'.

Good depth from the withers to behind the elbow is important, as are well-sprung ribs. Slab-sided horses are also difficult to keep in condition. (Note, though, that narrow chests, slab sides and cow hocks can result from poor feeding in early years, so a weedy mare may well be capable of breeding a foal that is far better than herself.) The back should dip gently; a roach back, straight or even bowed upwards, generally goes with a poor ribcage. Old ponies often have dipped backs, but in younger ones this may be a sign of having

40

carried too much weight. A 'good top line' is a series of gentle curves from poll to dock, not straight lines awkwardly joined.

A very long-backed pony finds it difficult to collect himself and can be weak in the loin. However, a reasonably long back is a guarantee of a comfortable ride and good reach at the gallop. The shorter the back the more athletic and manoeuvrable the pony, for he finds it easy to get his hocks under him and make full use of the power of his hindquarters. In some ways this manoeuvrability makes a very short-backed pony less suitable as a novice ride since he can change direction in a single stride even at top speed. Arabs are short-backed because they have one less vertebra, and both they and part-Arabs are far stronger in the back than other similar ponies. On the whole a short back gives greater stamina.

The hindquarters are the horse's engine and the more powerful they are the better. The depth from front to back, taken from the point of the hip to the back of the buttock, and the width when seen from behind affect the amount of muscle, and therefore the pushing power, of the pony. In Arabs the hindquarters are flatter on top and deep from front to back, almost triangular in shape; in cobs they are rounder and the hips broader. A good cob has 'a head like the lady's maid and a bottom like the cook's'. A high-set tail is generally favoured although in the cobs it is typically lower.

From behind, the back legs should be straight and square. The hocks should be generous and strong: a pony with poor hocks cannot perform well. From the side, the point of the hock should be level with the back of the buttock and the cannon bone fall vertically below the hock: sickle hocks, which are overbent so that the cannon bone is set at an angle forward, are weak and liable to give trouble, while a horse with too straight a hock is unable to develop his full power. From behind, the back legs should be straight. Cow hocks, in which the cannon bone and foot turn out, and bow hocks, in which they turn in, are both weak. Cow hocks in an underfed youngster will usually straighten if the feet are trimmed regularly and carefully.

The hind pastern and foot should ideally be slightly more upright than the front: 55° rather than 50°. The hind foot is more oval than round.

41

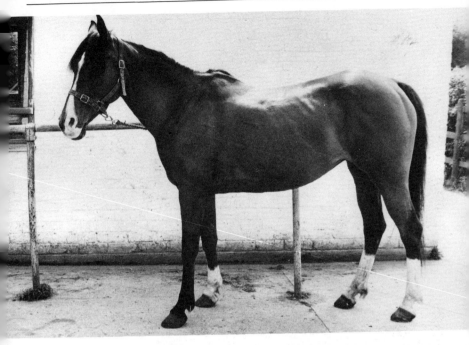

Partbred pony about 14.1 hands. This pony is very underweight: note the poverty streaks on her hindquarters and the lack of flesh on her neck and back. However she looks healthy and free of worms so her thinness is probably due to underfeeding, teeth problems, being bullied or prolonged stress. Her head seems too big, her back too long and her hindquarter weak, though these points will improve greatly as she gets fatter. She has a short, rather ewe-shaped neck which might improve; her rather straight shoulder will not. As she stands her best points are good withers, strong clean legs, good pasterns and well-shaped, well-shod feet.

Good feeding will improve this pony's appearance immeasurably and she will make a good all-round pony

Good quality cob pony with dreadful back legs. He is cow-hocked and also too straight in the hock. Such a pony cannot collect himself well, since he cannot carry himself with his hocks under him. Instead he moves with his hocks strung out behind, usually moving wide. Despite his excellent conformation in front – head, neck, shoulder and chest are splendid – he will never make a good riding pony

43

Welsh section C champion Leyeswick Flyer in magnificent condition, fat for the show ring but rippling with muscle. He has a real stallion's crest, a pretty pony head and superb laid-back shoulder; very good legs, pasterns and feet and strong hindquarters. He is rather low-backed but this often goes with the extremely high action he shows. He is wearing a show bridle and stallion bit (straight bar)

Effects of Condition on Appearance

A thin pony loses weight along the top line especially. The neck seems scrawnier, the head bigger, the back longer. A wormy pony will have a fat belly but be thin elsewhere; a starved one has no belly so it appears herring-gutted. The hindquarters will appear poor and the pony depressed. Good feeding will make great improvements but they will take months.

A well-fed pony usually reaches his full height around three and a half years old but fills out a little afterwards. A pony that has been consistently underfed when young will grow and improve for a full two years after this age if well fed.

A fat pony usually appears better than she really is, with a cresty neck and full hindquarters. A short neck is accentuated by fat.

Any pony's appearance improves with regular exercise.

6 Breeds and Types

Native Breeds

In the British Isles there are ten native breeds, more than in any other country. They are all hardy: on their native moors and mountains many still roam freely without any particular care or shelter. Unless overbred, they are sensible, surefooted and intelligent, and most are capable of carrying a good weight. Without doubt a native pony remains the most reliable choice for a novice rider.

All British breeds have a stud book in which pure-bred ponies are registered. Papers give the pony's pedigree and date of birth. However, unregistered pure-bred ponies off the moor may be quite as good as registered ones, and cheaper, though you may not be able to show one in a pure-bred class.

Connemara (13–14 hands) A medium-weight pony from the west coast of Ireland. Grey, bay or black; sometimes dun or cream. Introduced Arab and possibly Spanish blood probably improved the original, heavier pony, but the breed is well standardized. Particularly known for a good riding shoulder, stamina and an exceptional temperament, sensible and intelligent. Connemaras jump well. Suitable for child or adult.

Dales (13–14.2 hands) A docile, strong, cobby pony from the east of the Pennines. Usually black or bay, with a thick mane and tail and feathered legs (hairy heels). Like the Fell pony except that this is the heavier, driving or weight-carrying type; they were originally bred as packponies for carrying lead. Especially useful as an all-round pony on a smallholding, being easy to train to all types of work.

Dartmoor (up to 12.2 hands) A very old breed of exceptionally strong ponies, quite capable of carrying an adult. Usually bay, black or brown. Particularly known for their long life, hardiness, surefootedness and pretty heads. Good children's pony. Dartmoors are still bred on the moor but are also bred elsewhere. Some used to be crossed with Shetlands for pit ponies; this type is heavier and coarser, losing the lovely head.

Exmoor (up to 12.2 hands)   The most unchanged breed from earliest times. On the moor life is hard in winter, and moor-bred ponies are exceptionally hardy, very strong and definitely wild at first. Once tamed, they make excellent and vigorous family ponies. All have a characteristic mealy (oatmeal-coloured) nose and toad eyes: large, lovely eyes surrounded by a mealy-coloured ring. They are all a yellowish bay, dun or brown, with paler shading underneath; no white markings. The coat is unlike that of other breeds, having a waterproof outer layer in winter.

Fell (13–14 hands)   A solid, steady, ride-and-drive or trekking pony, ideal for a novice adult. From the west of the Pennines, they are lighter than the Dales ponies but still have feather and a good mane and tail. Usually black, sometimes brown; very true to type. A hardy and determined pony, a little heavy in hand unless well ridden.

Highland (12.2–14.2 hands)   The smaller ponies come from Barra and the outer islands. Very strong, docile, cobby ponies. Surefooted, often a bit heavy to ride but a good adult's pony. Pretty head, very broad, with bright eyes (probably improved by a dash of Arab blood long ago). Lovely colours – dark chestnut with silver mane and tail, dun with black dorsal stripe, grey, black and brown. Thick mane and tail.

New Forest (12–14.2 hands)   Ponies have been running in the Forest for at least a thousand years and many different stallions have been introduced, so the breed varies. Noted for a good riding shoulder, though bad ones are rather common-looking, with drooping hindquarters. Surefooted, docile, friendly and easier to break than other breeds living wild, they are good children's or all-round family ponies. Any colour except skewbald and piebald.

Shetland (up to 42 inches; 10.2h but Shetlands are measured in inches. Miniature Shetlands are even smaller – 36 inches maximum) Amazingly strong for their size, they are gentle and stolid. Exceptionally hardy, they are balls of fur in winter. Charming as pets, they can be wonderful for small children, but unless well trained they are far too headstrong for a child to control. Good driving ponies: this is one way to keep them obedient.

Welsh Mountain, Welsh Section A (11–12.2 hands)   The prettiest and gayest of all ponies, with a dished, Arab-type head, beautiful eyes, tiny ears, a high tail and great spirit. Good bone, excellent feet and high action. Wonderful gymkhana ponies, they drive well too, but their intelligence and dash, especially when young, may be too much for a nervous child.

Welsh Section B (12.2–13.2 hands)   These used to be the oversize Section A but most have now lost type, becoming a show-type pony with low action, rather like a small Thoroughbred. Lighter bone and less spirit than a true Welsh type.

Welsh Section C (up to 13.2 hands)   Undersized cobs but of true Welsh cob type.

Welsh Cob, Welsh Section D (13.2–15 hands)   Unlike what is generally termed a cob in England, good Welsh cobs are not dull, stolid beasts but spirited and lively ones, famed for their tremendous trot and high action. They have a broad, pony head, showing great intelligence and a touch of Arab way back. Most colours except piebald and skewbald, including palomino; seldom grey. Their boldness and kind, forgiving nature make them easy for a novice to handle despite their strength and spirit. An excellent all-round pony, up to any weight, the Welsh cob will ride, drive, plough, hunt; in short, do anything you might want a horse to do.

Other Breeds and Types

Arab   Arab horses have greatly improved the quality and looks of many other breeds, for they are the loveliest of all horses, with a fine, dished face, huge eyes, high tail carriage and floating action (though bad Arabs are the weediest, meanest, most useless creatures out). They are renowned for their stamina, gentleness and sensitivity. However, this sensitivity and their flightiness is exactly what makes them generally unsuitable for a novice. Arabs must trust you or they easily become nervous and panicky. They are unforgiving, never forgetting a mistake or pain, and they readily 'hot up' (get overexcitable). They are not hardy, having evolved in the desert, but they are very fast and manoeuvrable. On the whole they lack the boldness needed to jump well, but excel in endurance competitions. Except for Polish Arabs, they are not large: 14.2–15 hands.

Crossing an Arab with a native pony mare, particularly a Highland or Welsh cob, lightens what might otherwise be rather too heavy and stolid a pony for a rider with some experience. The Arab gives dash, speed, stamina and good looks; the native pony contributes hardiness, boldness, sense and a more forgiving nature. This type makes an excellent second pony.

Thoroughbred   Thoroughbreds were originally bred from Arabs to produce racehorses. They are tall, fine-skinned, bold animals with an excitable nature and an exceptional shoulder. Like Arabs, they cross well with the larger native ponies (the Thoroughbred–Connemara cross is particularly successful) to give a larger, faster pony. Show ponies generally have a good deal of Thoroughbred blood.

Thoroughbreds have delicate skin, a poor coat, lack the excellent hard feet of the Arab and in general are far more difficult to keep than any other breed. Any pony with Thoroughbred blood will inherit some of these characteristics along with the lovely head, shoulder and quality.

Cobs   Except for the Welsh ones, cobs are not a breed but a type: heavy-boned, sensible and easy to keep. A good cob is a jolly sort, game, unflappable, a great eater, and so steady-moving as to be hard to fall off, even bareback. A bad cob is heavy to ride, dull, ugly and so greedy he will knock you down to get at his food. Cobs are great all-round ponies, for driving and working as well as riding, but they tend to have a lumbering gallop and to lack sensitivity.

Coloured ponies (piebald and skewbald)   These colours are not allowed in the native breeds except the Shetland, but they are much favoured by gypsy breeders, probably because of the qualities they so often bring with them: honesty, great stamina and an enormous capacity for hard work. Coloured ponies are usually cobby, often with feather, not renowned for good looks, and sweet-tempered; but if you have one, be prepared to put up with a good deal of scorn from ignorant snobs.

Donkeys   Donkeys are as endearing to ponies as to people. Most are sweet-natured but can be maddening, being intelligent, strong-minded and peculiarly timid. A few (mostly jacks) are evil-tempered. Donkeys thrive on very little feed but, coming from desert mountains, are not suited to wet. The coat is not waterproof so they need shelter in winter. Their hooves grow very fast and are soft, so they need good care or regular roadwork to keep them down.

A well-trained donkey is rare but a safe, steady ride for a small child. Unless a proper donkey saddle or small Western saddle is used the child will tend to fall forward, for donkeys have a flat back, no withers or shoulder to speak of, and a low head carriage. They drive well and are great pack animals.

Donkeys carry lungworm, so they, and any ponies with them, need worming with ivermectin.

7 Buying a Pony

Buying a pony, like buying a second-hand car, can be disastrous or delightful, but there are obvious pitfalls the novice buyer can avoid.

First, consider seriously the amount of work and money involved so that you do not find yourself reselling or starving the pony in winter. Unfortunately it is not easy to give hard and fast rules about costs as these vary greatly with circumstances. A pony will make do on good grazing and a few supplementary feeds in summer; in winter (say twenty weeks in the south, thirty in the north) he will need hay and concentrates at least once a day. In severe weather he will need feeding twice a day. However, a native pony on good sheltered grazing will need literally quarter the feed that a blood pony in an exposed place on poor grazing does. Feeding requires organization and dedication as well as money. A feed missed in winter means weight lost; weight lost in winter is seldom regained before spring; and a thin pony has a far harder winter than a fat one. You will have to turn out twice a day in sleet and snow. Be sure, too, that you have a reliable back-up for times you go away or fall ill.

It is often possible to borrow a pony from a riding school or trekking centre for the winter in exchange for the keep. Such ponies are generally rather insensitive but bombproof. Borrowing a pony is an excellent way to find out how much work and money are involved over winter. Generally such ponies are returned at Easter. It is also possible to lease a pony, but consider carefully the problems arising from an accident or a serious illness.

Do ask other pony owners or your local riding school about the costs of feeding considering your grazing. It is a great help to find an experienced person whose opinion you respect, and who will in turn respect your eagerness to learn.

To your running costs add the cost of worming two to eight times a year; insurance and inoculations; a couple of vet's visits (with luck you will avoid this); and shoeing or trimming two to eight times a year. To the initial cost of the pony add the cost of a saddle, a bridle, a good bit and a basic grooming kit as minimum. Halters, lead ropes and haynets can be made. (See chapter 27.) A New Zealand rug will help a non-native pony.

Having worked out the costs, consider the type of pony you want. Native ponies and cobs are far hardier, cheaper and easier to keep than blood ponies such as Thoroughbred and Arab types. They are also less fidgety and flighty. Consider the suitability of every pony you see until you have built up a mental picture of what you want.

What size? By and large a strong 14.2 pony will carry all but the largest adults. In England there is a foolish prejudice towards having horses far larger than necessary. A pony is more agile and cheaper both to buy and to keep. Do not buy a child's pony larger than the child can comfortably handle.

What age? On the whole a middle-aged pony is most suitable for a novice, though there are great exceptions. As well as being more sensible, older ponies can be more evasive, wiser in the worst ways, quicker to take advantage, and harder-mouthed than younger ones. As a rough guide, a four-year-old will lack experience, especially in jumping and school work, but if he has been kindly broken he will be trusting and sensitive; if not he will be nervous and unreliable. At seven or eight a pony is mature physically and mentally, just entering his prime of life. Given the chance he will continue learning and improving for the next seven to ten years. With a little more coddling and care he will be good for another seven to ten years, though he will slow down. The useful age of a pony depends a great deal on how he has been kept and worked: some are old at fifteen, some at thirty. (My own first pony, a 12-hand Dartmoor, was given to me as an obstreperous and lively twenty-five-year-old. She was hunted regularly for five years, had her first, unexpected, foal at thirty-one and died at thirty-seven.)

Pure bred native ponies of the old-fashioned type may live to great ages and when old are usually wonderful for small or timid children. Many people will refuse to sell such an old granny but will lend or lease her to a kind home for years, a good arrangement if both parties have considered what to do if senility sets in.

What sex? Geldings are generally more even-tempered than mares. Only very few mares are really temperamental; more are a little silly in company, and pushy when handled, for a couple of days when in season (every three weeks throughout spring and summer). A good native mare that has already bred is an interesting proposition as a child's first pony as she can breed a second, larger pony for later.

When buying for a child, be aware that children who have only ridden at riding schools tend to think they ride better than they do and tend to know little about handling and keeping ponies. Riding-school ponies are chosen for their safety and they do a routine job well; privately owned ponies are generally livelier and more idiosyncratic, as well as more sensitive.

Price varies with size, type, breeding, age, performance, time of year and part of the country. To get an idea of fair prices go to your local horse sale, preferably without your chequebook. Ponies are relatively cheap at sales, the lowest bids being the meat price, but buying from a sale is a professional's job. There is no guarantee of behaviour, and many apparently quiet ponies bought at sales have turned out to be mad and uncatchable once at home. Especially where children are concerned, the risk, both physical and emotional, of such mistakes makes sales unsuitable places at which to buy, though you can learn a great deal there. The exceptions are the breed sales and those near native pony breeding areas, where healthy untouched youngsters are sold regularly.

To find a reliable pony, the farrier, the Pony Club and other horse owners are the best sources of information. A good riding school or dealer may also have something suitable, though riding school ponies tend to be hard-mouthed and some dealers still, alas, not wholly reliable. Horse magazines and the local paper are worth consulting, but word of mouth remains the best source.

If you are a novice you must have a reliable adviser. By all means make a preliminary visit yourself, but do not buy without independent experienced advice. It is usual to ask for a veterinary check too. The vet can guarantee the pony's health and soundness at the time of sale, but he cannot be asked to advise on character, behaviour and general suitability.

When arranging to see the pony, ask what it has been used for as well as its height, age and so on.

When you first see the pony, try to get an overall impression before beginning to judge him more carefully. Do you instantly like him? (No use asking a child this: children almost invariably like any pony they might be given.) Is he bright, interested, friendly, alert?

Check age and conformation as far as you are able to. Make sure the legs are straight and square. Ask the owner to lead or ride him towards and away from you. Does he move straight or does he throw one or more legs sideways? Look at the feet for horizontal marks on the inside coronet or on the flesh just above. These marks, seen especially on the hind feet, are made by the inside edge of one foot hitting the other foot as it swings forwards and show a bad defect in movement. Does the pony move freely, picking his feet up well? Old ponies get pottery, but pottery movement in others is unwelcome.

Are there patches of white hair on the withers or back? These result from saddle galls and their history should be discussed. Are there any other scars?

Now handle the pony. Give him a titbit, stroke his neck, lead him a few steps, stand him still. Does he welcome your attention? Is he willing? Calm?

Pick up a front foot. The shoe should be evenly worn, not scuffed at the front or lopsided. Uneven wear is a sign of bad action, bad conformation or bad shoeing. Are the hooves smooth, or do they have laminitis ridges? Ridges may be due to a change of food, but laminitis feet have a flat sole and weak heel and frog.

Pick up a back foot. Does the pony resist? Do you feel comfortable with it? Take the tail in one hand near the top and move it gently. The pony should be quite relaxed, not afraid of your handling his tail.

Examine the legs carefully, feeling all the way down them. There are many lumps and bumps that appear as a result of strain: hard bony ones like splints, bone spavin (hocks), ringbone and sidebone; soft ones like bog spavin, thoroughpin and windgalls; other irregular ones due to blows. It is difficult to remember them all but one good rule is that the legs should match. Some horses, for instance, have big bony knees or hocks (good), but if you suspect they are deformed due to strain, remember that strain seldom affects both legs equally: if they match they were probably made that way. Similarly the feet should match. Odd feet are very suspect.

Ask to see the pony ridden before you try yourself. Does he seem willing? Do you like the way he moves? When you try yourself be aware that most ponies behave differently in their own field from the way they do out on a ride. They are usually more wilful and sluggish at home. The pony will probably not go quite as well for you, a stranger, as for someone he is used to. If you do not seem to get on well together, ask the seller how to get the best out of him. Different ponies like to be ridden in slightly different styles, so you may have to make some adjustments. Only very experienced riders can feel what these adjustments should be within minutes of getting on a new pony, so do not be afraid to ask. Even if you and the pony click, it will probably be a couple of months before you achieve the best you can manage together, so remember things are fairly certain to improve. However, do not buy a pony that frightens you: this usually spells doom at some point in the future.

If no one is with you and you like the pony at this stage, say so and ask to come again. A genuine seller will not expect you to make up your mind instantly. However, if the pony is not for you, you should say so. If you find it difficult face to face, ring up later the same day. Nothing is more upsetting to a seller than an enthusiastic-sounding buyer who fails to reappear.

You will not be able to be sure of your judgement on all the above points, but you should watch to see your adviser checks them too. In particular, make sure the feet and lower legs are healthy: 'No foot, no 'oss.'

If the pony was already saddled and bridled the first time you saw him, try to make sure that on your second visit you see him in the field, catch him and bridle him yourself. Some ponies are hard to catch. You can usually alter this but it takes a great deal of time and patience.

Ask if you can go out for a short ride, especially on the road to check his behaviour in traffic.

Some owners may allow you to take the pony on trial. Do so only in good faith and only when you have both considered who takes responsibility in case of an accident.

When you take the pony home, allow him to settle for a day before riding him out.

8 Feed and Feeding

Horses have small stomachs for their size. Their digestive system is designed to cope with a steady input of at least eight feeding sessions a day, unlike that of a dog or cat, which can stuff itself every two days and remain healthy. Wild ponies on the usual unlimited poor grazing eat for a couple of hours and rest for a couple of hours alternately throughout the day and most of the night. They grow fat in summer, reaching top weight in autumn, and living off it all winter. By spring their ribs show, but by then the new grass comes through. Despite this huge variation in bodyweight each year – a quarter or so of the animal's weight is lost and made up – horses remain healthy. They get a certain amount of exercise as they live in rough, uneven country, but they are never superfit.

When we keep and feed ponies we try to keep the bodyweight more constant, since we want them to maintain their fitness rather than puffing fatly one month and being skinnily exhausted another. We keep them free from parasites and look after their teeth, so that they can use their food better, and we give them better-quality food. In exchange we demand a certain amount of work.

How much should you feed? There can only be guidelines, not hard-and-fast rules, for ponies' needs vary widely. Height, breed, time of year, grazing, amount of work, shelter and even character affect their food requirements. These guidelines are for a pony on minimal or no grazing, i.e. in winter or stabled.

Guideline Quantities for Feeding: Daily Rations

Height	Approxi-mate weight	Maintenance (good hay)	Light work (concentrates)	Hard work (concentrates)
12 h	400 lb	6 lb	2 lb	4 lb
13 h	600 lb	9 lb	3 lb	6 lb
14 h	800 lb	12 lb	4 lb	8 lb
15 h	1000 lb	15 lb	5 lb	10 lb

Notes

These rations are calculated as 1.5 per cent of the pony's bodyweight in hay for maintenance. If you are interested you can obtain a weight tape, which measures your pony's girth and gives his approximate weight.

If the pony is exposed in winter, increase the amount of hay. Most bales weigh 40–50 lb, so a 14 hand pony should have about a quarter to a third of a bale a day, more in hard weather.

Calculate your winter's hay needs as follows: the daily requirement for a 14 hand pony is about 12 lb and there are 180 days (6 months) in a winter. Therefore the total winter's feed = $12 \times 180 = 2160$ lb. One ton (2240 lb) will be ample. In the south, with good sheltered grazing, you would need considerably less; in the snowy north you might run short. In an average week you would use two bales. Start offering hay at half this rate in November, building up over a month to a third of a bale a day. Feed more when the ground is snow-covered: a full belly keeps the cold out.

For concentrates, coarse mix or nuts are the easiest to feed. You can replace half the ration with sugarbeet (weigh dry). Oats give pep, barley warmth.

Light work means weekend riding; hard work an average of one to two hours daily. As a pony gets fitter he will do more work for the same ration.

Succulents, carrots, swede, turnip, apples, etc. add bulk, fibre and vitamins but do not greatly increase a pony's energy or protein intake.

Having started with the guideline quantities you may find your pony needs up to a quarter more or less. He may also prefer some foods to others.

The golden rules of feeding, then, are:

*1 **Feed by eye*** If the pony is losing weight, feed more; if getting fat, feed less. Do not assume that she must do well on the guideline quantities. Use sense, not rules.

You should always run your hand over your pony in winter when you feed her, no matter how rushed you are. Shaggy winter coats cover ribbiness; it is not always obvious to any but an expert eye that anything is wrong. Put one hand on the pony's chest and feel the backbone and ribs with the other. The spine should not stick up, nor should the bones of the chest protrude. You should only just be able to feel the ribs when you rub your hand firmly over them.

The neck is the first part to lose weight, followed by the rump. Develop a critical eye for these areas. An underfed pony is likely to be bad-tempered and to feel dull and lifeless when ridden.

Overfeeding is as easy as underfeeding and perhaps more injurious to the pony's health. It is not kind to keep a pony rolling fat: laminitis, heart and tendon strain and azoturia (see page 212) all result from too much rich food. So does over-energetic and overexcitable behaviour, especially when the pony is fit and stabled.

*2 **Feed little and often*** As the pony's stomach is small, feeds should not be more than half a 2-gallon bucket for a large pony or quarter of a bucket for a small pony. At grass, ponies are better fed twice a day in winter, three times in hard weather. A stabled pony should be fed at least four times a day if stress, which can lead to colic and bad behaviour, is to be avoided.

*3 **Feed plenty of roughage*** A pony's digestive system is not designed to cope with concentrated food. Roughage is especially important to a stabled pony to prevent constipation, colic and stable vices. A pony will not gorge himself on hay as he will on concentrates. Do not fear that by feeding concentrates and hay at the same time you are breaking rule 2 above.

4 Water before feeding   After a long day a thirsty pony can drink 2 or 3 gallons of water. If he does this on a full stomach, food can be washed into the next part of the gut, causing irritation and colic. Leave a thirsty pony quietly with his water for five or ten minutes before even hinting that food is on its way. If he will not drink or if he takes a couple of swallows after eating to wash his mouth out, don't panic. It is the effect of large quantities of water on top of freshly eaten food that is the trouble.

Do not allow a hot pony to drink a lot of very cold water at once; cool the pony, warm the water, or give him small quantities at five-minute intervals.

5 Do not work a pony on a full stomach   As a general rule feed at least an hour before exercise. Do not expect a pony to go at more than a walk for an hour after finishing his feed. Do not allow him to drink a large amount and then gallop violently. On a long day, for instance, out hunting, you are best allowing the pony to drink small quantities whenever he wants so he never builds up a thirst.

6 Never feed poor-quality foodstuffs   Any kind of upset stomach is bound to cause colic as a pony cannot be sick. Mouldy nuts and foul-smelling oats must not be fed. Musty hay contains spores which affect a pony's lungs, making him cough for months or years. If you are doubtful about some of your hay, soak a netful in a bath of water for twelve hours before feeding; sprinkle it with dilute molasses if the pony disapproves. Feeding any but the best-quality hay to a stabled horse is asking for trouble.

7 Do not change the food suddenly   Allow a few days' transition when you should mix the new type with the old in gradually increasing quantities. This is particularly important if you bring a pony in to constant stabling after being out. The change from fresh food to dry concentrates may often cause colic due to a blockage since the pony may stuff himself. Make the change gradual. The reverse happens when a stabled pony is turned out on spring grazing: diarrhoea will result unless the change is gradual.

58

Glossary of Foodstuffs

A = *additives*   Additives should be fed in small quantities to increase mineral and vitamin intake. Those listed here are mostly cheap and old-fashioned; there are many modern branded additives on the market at far greater cost. They are usually used for stabled horses or as a tonic. Some succulents are also classed as additives as they do not form the major part of a pony's diet.

B = *bulk feed*   These give necessary roughage as well as having nutritional value.

C = *concentrates*   Concentrates are high in nutritional value but low in roughage.

Alfalfa (lucerne) (B)   Dried alfalfa has an extremely high food value as well as providing good roughage. Difficult to get. Slight mineral imbalance: if fed as the major or only food source alfalfa must be balanced by a phosphorus-rich additive.

Apples (A)   Not only a treat: apples are a valuable succulent and will tempt a poor feeder.

Barley (C)   Fed crushed, micronized (steamed) or boiled whole, barley is a high-quality feed. It has a high carbohydrate content and is particularly suitable when a pony works long and slow (e.g. trekking), for a thin and/or cold pony, and as a winter feed. Whole barley is cheap in barley-growing areas but should be boiled, when its food value is greatly increased. A nightly feed of hot boiled barley is wonderful for an old or exposed pony in winter.

Beans (C)   Seldom fed alone nowadays but a major component of pony nuts. Heating (i.e. exciting). Fed boiled or dried, a handful only, field or broad beans have a high protein content.

Beer (A)   Stale beer and barrel-bottoms have a high yeast content and act as a tonic. Stout is rich in iron and used to be widely used in racing yards or in sickness.

Big bales   Half-hay, half-silage made in black plastic bags. Not suitable for horses.

Bran (C)   Traditionally bran was used as a cheap, laxative rest-day feed for hardworking stabled horses. However, modern milling robs bran of all its food value and as it positively removes minerals from other foods it is mixed with, it is now expensive and worthless.

Bread (B)   Brown bread and other baker's waste can be a useful food so long as they do not make up too great a proportion of the feed. Bread is a good titbit as it does not make ponies greedy. A sick animal will often take brown bread before other foods.

Carrots (B)   Tasty, succulent and rich in vitamin A. Where carrots are cheap, feed 3–6 lb daily for improved skin, glossy coat and good feet. They are excellent for stabled horses as they are a mild laxative.

Chaff (B)   Hay, straw and gorse used to be chaffed to bulk up the feed of stabled horses. Today molassed chaff is a welcome but expensive alternative, especially for ponies allergic to hay. It is well worth chaffing your own if you can find a chaff-cutter.

Coarse mix (C)   Horse muesli. A high-quality concentrate containing a balanced mixture of cereals and minerals with molasses. A good choice if you are only feeding one concentrate, and ponies love it. Do not buy it in bulk as it will go stale.

Corn oil (A)   A couple of tablespoons daily improves the coat.

Eggs (A)   An excellent old-fashioned tonic for improving condition and coat. One a day.

Flaked maize (C)   Too high in fat and low in protein to be the major concentrate source, but a handful will tempt a poor feeder.

Grass pellets (B)   A replacement for hay in the diet of a wheezy or allergic pony.

Hay (B)   Hay varies enormously in food value. The best is pale brown with a tinge of green and is made from the first growth of grass before it has gone stemmy and shed its seed. Mouldiness starts on the inside of a bale, so test hay by thrusting your hand right into the centre of the bale, grasping a handful and pulling it out to smell it. Good hay smells sweet and fresh. Make a habit of testing any hay you see and you will soon develop a good nose for it. Tight bales are more likely to be mouldy inside; loose bales fall to pieces when handled. On average there are around forty-five bales in a ton but there may be as few as thirty or as many as sixty.

Newly made hay is not good for ponies as it creates gas in the stomach which they cannot belch up (cows can). Conversely, ponies can eat year-old or even two-year-old hay, which is not fed to cattle. In fact, delicate ponies are better fed on year-old hay.

Seed hay is made from reseeded pasture, meadow hay from permanent pasture. The best meadow hay has a wider variety of herbs and grasses than seed hay and is more nutritious. However, poor meadow hay may contain not so palatable species and may even contain poisonous plants like ragwort, as will hay made from roadside verges.

Household waste (A, B, C) Save peelings of turnip, carrot, cabbage, apples, etc., to bulk up the feed and add vitamins and variety. Do not use onions, leeks or sprouts, or fish. Most ponies will not eat meat, but, cooked, it does them no harm. Sprouting or green potatoes are poisonous.

Linseed (A) A valuable traditional additive to fatten, put on condition, and particularly to add gloss to the coat. It is laxative. Feed once or twice weekly to a stabled pony. Simmer a handful of linseed in a couple of pints of water for two hours. The result is a gooey jelly which is added to the feed.

Milk powder/milk substitute (A) Far too high in protein for ordinary use, but half a cupful added to the feed of an emaciated pony, especially a youngster, will speed recovery.

Mineral or salt lick (A) Should always be available to a stabled pony.

Molasses (A) A real treat, useful for disguising sharp tastes, medicine, worming powders, and so on as well as tempting a finicky feeder or sick pony.

Nettles (A) A good source of minerals, especially iron. Use dried and chopped in a feed as a tonic and to improve the coat. Many ponies will eat wilted nettles readily. If your grazing has nettles, do not spray them but cut them a few at a time and let the pony pick at them as they dry.

Nuts/pony nuts/cubes (C) A balanced mixture of concentrates and minerals specially made for ponies. Nuts or coarse mix are the easiest concentrates to feed. Only buy a bag at a time, as they go stale with keeping. Mix with succulents for a greedy feeder. Some ponies do not seem to thrive on nuts.

Oats (C) High in protein, energy and calcium, good oats are the traditional basis of concentrate feeding. They are not suitable for children's ponies as they are heating, i.e. make the pony too excitable and energetic. Poor oats are thin, husky, dusty and of low value; good oats feel fat to the touch and smell rich. Dampen oats before feeding.

Seaweed (A) Rich in minerals. Seaweed improves the quality of the skin and the hardness of the hoof.

Silage (B) Great arguments rage about the advisability of feeding silage. Some people do so with great success; others find it causes colic, probably due to overacidity. Hardy native ponies running out seem to thrive on it; more delicate types, perhaps on a more restricted diet, may suffer. There seems to be no hard-and-fast rule except that poor-quality silage is bound to cause trouble. If you intend to feed silage, use only the best and feed cautiously and gradually, keeping a watchful eye on the results until you see whether it suits your pony. Do not assume that one batch of silage is the same as the next.

Straw (B) Eating straw can be a problem in stabled ponies as gorging on new straw can cause impaction colic. However, feed (barley) straw is nutritious and rich in fibre, and can be used as a bulk feed to supplement the hay ration of outdoor ponies, especially in hard weather. Only the best straw, bright and fresh-smelling, will be accepted. It has much less protein than hay and should be regarded as a 'fill-belly'. Modern methods of harvesting mean that awns are no longer a problem, as used to be the case.

Sugarbeet (B, C) Dried sugarbeet pulp is a high-energy, low-protein concentrate and is an ideal feed for ponies. It must be soaked before feeding or it can cause choking or colic. Cover with water and allow an extra couple of inches of water on top; leave overnight or for a maximum of a day, but no longer or it starts to ferment, especially in hot weather. Beet nuts take three times their own volume of water and need soaking for twenty-four hours. For a treat on a cold winter's night use boiling water on beet pulp, cover, leave in a warm place for forty minutes, and feed warm mixed with barley. Fresh beets are sugar-rich and a real treat.

Turnips and swedes (A, B) These are good succulents, used to bulk out the feed. They have little food value but can be used in quantity to supplement a short hay ration.

Vitamins (A) Ponies fed on good mixed grazing, balanced concentrates and hay are unlikely to be short of vitamins. Vitamin A deficiency shows in a poor coat and bad vision, and is cured by the liberal feeding of carrots. The B vitamins are needed for efficient use of food. A vitamin B-deficient pony not only uses its food less well but also loses its appetite, so it goes downhill more and more. Eating dead bracken causes vitamin B deficiency. Any really unthrifty pony is almost certainly B-deficient and should be given yeast (see next page). Vitamin C is present in greenstuff, hence the need for fresh food in a stabled horse. It is necessary for rapid healing, resistance to infection and healthy skin. Vitamin D is derived from sunlight. Vitamin E, necessary for good fertility, is also present in greens.

Yeast (A)   An excellent, cheap source of vitamin B. Use ½–1 oz daily (a lump the size of a small egg if using fresh yeast) mixed in feed or in treacle.

BEWARE of: hay made from roadside verges. It may contain poisonous plants, for example ragwort, which ponies will take when dried; lawn clippings, which tend to start fermenting and can be full of weedkiller and yew. If you are certain they are safe, feed only handfuls at a time.

STORAGE: Keep your feed in rat-proof, damp-proof containers. Plastic dustbins are ideal; old deep-freezes are also good but prop the lid open a fraction or there will be condensation. Damp food goes mouldy fast. It is not a good idea to buy a lot of food at once.

Hay should be stacked under cover. Put pallets or poles on the ground to keep air flowing under the bottom layer, even if the ground is dry. Stack the bottom layer on edge to minimize spoilage. It is usually cheaper to buy hay straight from the field if you can store it. Bales vary in size, so ask how many go to the ton. There will be a small weight loss due to drying if the hay is absolutely fresh.

Special Feeding

Thin pony

Check teeth for sharpness (particularly in older ponies) or changing teeth (particularly in younger ponies). Dropping the food while eating (quidding), getting a food ball in the cheek or making strange yawning faces when trying to clean lumps of food off the teeth may all be indications of sharp teeth.

Worm. Thin ribs, a fat belly, tail-scratching and general unthriftiness are especial signs of worms.

Suspect also a shortage of water or grazing, increase of work, bullying, general nervousness or unhappiness.

Increase the number of feeds rather than the size of them. Boiled barley, yeast, linseed, sugarbeet, flaked maize and good mixed grazing will help fatten a pony. Light exercise stimulates the appetite: most ponies will not put on weight if kept stabled and unexercised.

Fat pony

A fat pony is in bad condition, liable to get laminitis, strained tendons, heart strain and wind trouble. Slim by reducing the amount of feed and grazing (either tether the pony or keep him in a poor paddock) or by keeping him inside overnight without food. If you keep him in, use uneatable bedding and high-bulk feed such as chaffed straw and turnips.

A pony that has had laminitis should be thin in April. Do not be foolishly tenderhearted about this: laminitis is appallingly painful and damaging.

General unthriftiness

If the pony is wormed and well fed, suspect mineral imbalance, vitamin B deficiency, bracken or ragwort poisoning. Use proprietary supplements or yeast, linseed, molasses, chopped wilted nettles, seaweed and a mineral lick.

Finicky feeder

Yeast stimulates the appetite; so does exercise. Feed little and often, tempt with molasses, sliced carrot, flaked maize and apples. Examine her teeth and mouth carefully.

Greedy feeder

A pony that bolts his nuts may choke. Slow down his eating by mixing in chaff, chopped vegetables and sugarbeet or by putting a large round stone in his feed pot.

Poor hooves

Feed a Biotin-rich supplement and seaweed powder.

Heaves (COPD, hay fever/allergy)

A stabled pony must be kept on bedding other than straw. Feed best silage, sugarbeet and succulents for bulk. Grass pellets and dust-free haylage (very expensive) are also useful. Sugarbeet can be fed in large quantities, making up the pony's staple feed as long as bran is fed as well to balance the pony's mineral intake. However, some ponies scour (get diarrhoea) on this mixture, so increase the sugarbeet gradually.

A pony that suffers from COPD is best kept outside. (See also page 215.)

9 Keeping a Pony at Grass

Given plenty of rough grazing and mild winters, ponies are perfectly capable of looking after themselves. It is only when we limit their range and choices that we have to take care of them.

If you watch a pony grazing along a weed-infested verge you will see that she chooses many other plants besides grass: leaves, twigs and bark of trees, brambles, gorse and thistles, young rushes and cow parsley. Many of these contain minerals and trace elements the pony needs, and she keeps herself in good health when allowed these choices. The best grazing for ponies is not flat acres of reseeded rye grass and clover, which make them fat but soft; it is old, mixed grazing with trees, hedges and even marsh.

How much land is necessary? It depends, of course, on the quality of grazing, the size of pony, the shelter and aspect. A couple of acres is about the minimum for anything but a tiny pony. If you only have one field you will have to practise grassland management.

Ponies do not like to live alone. Organize company for your pony. Consider arranging with someone else to keep your pony with theirs, alternating between your field and theirs. Or you could give a home to a tiny or old pony or a donkey, calf, goat or sheep for company. Loneliness is real to a pony, and a happy pony is easier to keep and less likely to get into trouble than a miserable one.

Having secured adequate grazing, check the following:

Fencing   Good hedges are by far the best form of fencing, offering mixed browsing and shelter. If you are intending to continue keeping ponies, consider planting a hedge, but remember that ponies love to eat young beech. Walls are also good, providing shelter from driving winds and rain. Posts and rails make safe, secure fencing. New wire

65

fencing should be plain, not barbed. Any existing barbed wire must be really tight. Barbed-wire cuts fester easily, and ponies that get caught in sagging barbed-wire fences often die from their injuries. Sheep netting can cause problems as many ponies paw the fence while waiting for food and may get a leg, or more usually a shoe, caught. You can prevent this by nailing planks inside the fence.

Water   There must be a supply of fresh water. If there is no stream, the best container is a plastic dustbin, which is easy to empty and wash out. Ponies can knock their knees against the upturned rim of an old bath. Buckets do not hold enough water unless you have a row of them, and they are too easily knocked over.

Keep the water container clean. Standing water goes stale quickly and the pony may refuse to drink it, giving you the impression he has plenty to drink when in fact he has nothing acceptable. If your pony has water in the field but always tries to drink when out on a ride, ask yourself why before getting annoyed.

Poisonous plants   Yew is deadly. Ponies do not normally eat it, but they will when hungry or when the ground is snow-covered. They will also graze under yew trees and may pick up enough fallen leaves to be poisoned.

Ragwort contains a deadly, slow-acting poison that destroys the liver so that the pony starts ailing mysteriously and slowly. There is no cure. Ponies will not eat fresh ragwort but they will take it dry in hay, and in autumn they pick up fallen leaves by grazing under plants. Many fatal cases occur in ponies that have lived in ragwort-infested fields in apparent safety for years, the effects not being noticeable until too late. Pull up any ragwort plants and burn them.

Bracken, eaten when wilting, causes vitamin B deficiency, but ponies are not susceptible to the type of bracken poisoning that cows get. Privet, lupins and autumn crocus are poisonous and are eaten fresh; deadly nightshade is not eaten fresh but may be taken dried in hay. Unripe acorns can cause severe colic. Laburnum is also poisonous but seldom eaten.

Rubbish   Never put a pony out in a new field without checking for rubbish first, even if there are other ponies there that have learned to pick their way round litter.

Feeding Arrangements

For each pony you will need a bucket or feed pot. Old earthenware sinks or boxes attached to the fence make good feed pots as they cannot be knocked over. If a pony paws the bucket when he eats, put it in the middle of an old car tyre; if you hang it on the fence he will probably paw the fence.

Feed hay in a rack or a haynet. If you are making a rack, make it movable. Haynets come in various sizes – hunter, cob, pony; you can also make them easily out of bale string.

Feeding at Grass

The first grass of spring is better food value than anything you can buy, full of protein and vitamins; the value then decreases gradually through the summer but rises again with the autumn flush (September). From November on the food value in grass drops to virtually nil, though there may still be plenty of bulk there.

Unless he is being worked extremely hard or is on very poor grazing, your pony will need no extra feed during summer and autumn. After a long hard day, a rally or a show, give a feed of concentrates (2 lb for a small pony, 4–6 lb for a large one (see chapter 8)) and chopped vegetables; you may also like to give a feed before starting. You are the best judge as to whether your pony needs these extra feeds in summer. If he starts to feel tired after weeks of work instead of getting livelier as he gets fitter, then he needs more food. However, a pony that has rested all winter will start lively, then get sluggish before he gets fit. This process will take some six weeks or so. For an equal amount of work a fit pony needs less food than an unfit one; there is no reason why this should not be provided by good grazing.

From the beginning of November start offering hay and concentrates at half the normal rate. In the south your grazing may last a little longer, but do not wait until the pony loses weight. Do not increase the rate of feeding until the pony is finishing his hay well. By Christmas you should be on winter rations.

Feed twice daily, half a ration at each feed, throughout the winter, and make the last feed as late as possible. In hard weather, with snow on the ground or continuous sleet or rain, you will need to feed an extra half ration of hay. He should be eating as much hay as he wants without wasting any. A constantly full stomach guards against cold and misery. If this involves a vast quantity of hay and an overfat pony, mix straw into the ration or offer it as well. It will not add greatly to the food value but it will fill his belly cheaply.

You may find your pony eating trees. This is not from starvation but from taste: some ponies, especially native ponies and cobs, love to eat trees when the sap is flowing strongly. They eat beech bark in autumn, ash in spring; they eat the leaves the other way round. It does the ponies nothing but good but will kill the trees unless you wrap them with sacking or wire.

As the weather eases off towards spring you can decrease the feed ration. Watch the roadside verges for signs of grass growing; you will not see it in the field as the pony will eat it as fast as it grows. New grass is as rich as concentrated feed. If in difficulty, reduce the concentrate ration rather than the bulk. In spring the best tonic is to take your pony out for an hour's grazing in a lush gateway or quiet lane. Later in the summer you will have to beware of this because in many areas the verges are sprayed. However, in spring new grass is as valuable as oats. You can also tether your pony in quiet areas. Many people have a rough area of garden or unfenced orchard which they are happy to have grazed by a tethered pony.

If your pony is of the real native sort and you fear laminitis, cut out concentrates altogether in March and aim to reduce her weight before the grass comes through. Do not be soft-hearted about this. You can still give a good feed of mixed vegetables and chaff if it makes you both feel better. You might also consider replacing some of her hay with straw if she seems hungry but is not losing weight: that is, reduce the food value without reducing the bulk.

Bullying

When keeping two or more ponies together never try to feed one in the field without feeding the others at the same time. Make sure that haynets and feed pots are far enough apart so that the ponies cannot kick one another even if they turn their rumps to one another. In most groups of ponies, one or more bullies will terrorize the others at feeding time, especially when they are cold and hungry. There may be one particular victim. You cannot argue with the bully: you have to change the feeding arrangements so the victim can get food without being frightened. Put out more feeding places than ponies, and have them well separated. Double-sided hay racks are a help.

Bullying may be the reason for one pony mysteriously losing weight. Watch your ponies while they feed – throughout the feed, not just for the first few minutes – and you will see if one is being cheated out of food.

Grassland Management

Ponies will not eat where they have dunged. They are choosy feeders, leaving some parts and grazing others flat, so that after a couple of years continuous grazing some parts of the field are overgrazed and others long and rank. As creeping buttercup readily invades overgrazed areas, the usable grazing gradually diminishes.

The only way round this problem is to manage your grassland before it gets pony-sick by either (a) removing all dung, (b) mixed-species grazing or (c) strip grazing.

Removing all the dung is only feasible if the area is small and you have a lot of time. Collect all dung daily, composting it carefully. Once rotted it can be reused as manure without the pony objecting, but it must rot down well for a year for the worm larvae to be killed. Lime the field well.

Mixed-species grazing is the easiest and best form of grassland management. Cows, sheep and geese eat ponies' dunged patches happily provided they are not years old and rank. One pony and one heifer do not take as much from the pasture as two ponies, for they eat different plants and eat each other's dung patches, so increasing the value of the grazing. There is also profit in raising a heifer. However, ponies graze lower than cows, so when the grazing gets short you may have to hand-feed a heifer. Sheep also graze short but are more difficult to fence; geese need housing every night.

The third alternative is to split the grazing into three paddocks and graze each one flat before starting the next. Manure and lime each paddock as the pony moves on. Harrowing spreads manure and

Good management. These ponies, all rather overweight, are kept with a cow who eats down the patches they leave, thus increasing the available grazing. Their large, well-placed shelter is open on two sides, protecting them from the prevailing wet south-westerlies while allowing a view. Solid walls and post and rail form the fencing

loosens tufts of rank grass; it is an excellent tonic in early spring and any sensible pony can be taught to pull a harrow without too much difficulty (see chapter 20).

You can use an electric fence for paddock grazing. A pony cannot see the thin wire that is used, so it is helpful to tie little bits of bright ribbon or string along it at first. Warn the pony of the danger by leading her to the fence, warning her by voice and action that you are afraid of it, before letting her touch it. Repeat this, praising her when she pulls away before touching the fence. Once she has been trained to a fence you will not have to leave the current on all the time. You

Bad management. This depressed pony lives alone in a small, shelterless field with poor fencing: saggy barbed wire looped carelessly round the post will cause an accident sooner or later. He has lice (see page 216) and has scratched his neck bare. The cold wind makes his eyes run. Although decently fed, he is thin, as the top of his neck and wither show. His poor condition is due more to misery and loneliness than lack of food

will also be able to make her believe that other wire is electrified by tying the same ribbons to it, but do not cry wolf too often or she will grow wise to it. Never put a pony in a field with an electric fence without warning her, for the first time she is shocked she may bolt through the fence and panic herself.

Whichever form of management you choose, at the end of winter you will need to cut any long rank grass and spread manure, fertilizer or lime. Harrow in early spring. Clean out your haybarn and use the sweepings of any muddy and bare patches to reseed them. Cut rushes in early spring, raking them off so the new growth, which ponies thrive on, can come through. Ponies will gradually clear a field of rushes but only if you take off all the old growth.

In spring and summer, weed out docks, ragwort and plantains. Bracken should be cut and raked off at least twice a year. Rotted, it makes valuable manure, but ponies get vitamin B deficiency from eating wilted bracken. Cut nettles a few at a time and let them lie, when the pony will eat them.

Shelter

A field shelter keeps food dry, gives a pony's back a chance to dry while he is eating, and provides shelter from flies. Apart from that, ponies will often refuse to stay in a shelter unless they are shut in. They are more likely to use an open-fronted shelter than a closed one.

If you decide to build a shelter do not be in too much of a hurry. Give yourself time to watch where the worst winds come from, which areas of the field drain well, and where the ponies choose to shelter. A badly placed shelter is worse than none at all, so let the ponies show you the best spot.

Make sure the shelter is plenty big enough, depending on the number and size of your ponies. Compare and measure other shelters. Consider using the roof space for storing hay; this will add to the warmth. Consider also leaving the front open or closing it only to half height. As long as they are dry ponies do not suffer much from cold, but they do get uneasy if their view is blocked.

Bricks or breeze blocks are the best material; creosoted wood cladding is also good. Corrugated iron is a popular but mistaken choice. Unless it is new and very carefully laid it will work loose and turn up at the corners, causing rattles, draughts and horrible injuries; moreover it holds no warmth. Old railway wagons are good but you may have to remove the floor or it will rot.

If the shelter is on well-drained soil and surrounded by drainage channels the earth floor will stay in good condition if a bale of straw or dry bracken is laid down. Do not muck out a field shelter but lay fresh bedding on top to build up a deep bed. If it will not keep dry, lay a rough floor sloping towards the front. Do not use hardcore; it works up into ponies' feet. Concrete, blocks or bricks are better.

New Zealand rug. This is of the type that does not need a surcingle. Bits of sheepskin have been sewn round the wither and neck areas to prevent rubbing

Rugs

A New Zealand rug is designed for continuous outdoor wear in winter. Hardy native ponies do not need to be rugged and many resent it, but more delicate ponies do benefit from the extra warmth. Old ponies of any type, especially if suffering from rheumatism, also welcome a rug. If your pony sweats heavily when exercised, you can clip him and put a rug on him (see page 127).

Start rugging up on cold nights in November, leaving the rug off whenever the days are warm and sunny; similarly, start leaving the rug off on warm spring days. If you leave the rug on the pony for long periods remove it every day to make sure it is not chafing. A poorly fitting rug can cause severe rubbing and will need padding with sheepskin or a similar material where it presses on the shoulders. A surcingle must have two pads separated by a gap on its under side where it passes over the back, so that there is no pressure directly on the backbone; on a cheap rug these may be missing. Do not fasten a surcingle tightly.

Never put a rug on a pony that is hot, sweating, wet or muddy. A wet pony can be 'thatched', that is, covered thickly with straw and a rug thrown loosely over the top. He will steam into the straw and dry himself.

Rewaterproof your rug every year; a wet rug is worse than none at all.

Headcollar

Do not turn your pony out in a headcollar unless she is so hard to catch that it is necessary. A foot or a branch may catch in it, causing injury. If you feel a headcollar is really necessary, fasten it with string that will easily break if the pony is in trouble.

10 Stabling

Mentally and physically a pony is designed to live outside, free, and the smaller the space he is shut in, the more of a strain it is. We are used to thinking of stables as the 'right' places for horses to be, but this is only because in our forefathers' days many horses had to be kept in stables as they worked in cities. Constant stabling puts tremendous stress on horses, so many books were written about the difficult art of keeping them healthy and happy when stabled. A smart stable yard full of shining horses pleases us, but if you learn to recognize the signs you will see that the majority of them would be far happier ambling about free and scruffy.

You should not, then, aim to keep your pony constantly stabled, although bad weather, sickness, injury or other circumstances may force you to do so for a while. However, if you are short of grazing, live in an exposed place or have a delicate pony, keeping him in at nights and out in the day during winter may benefit you both.

The In-and-Out System

The stable should be plenty large enough for the pony to walk around in. It must be airy: ponies suffer less from the cold than from stuffy air, which is particularly bad for their lungs when they cannot move around. (They do not mind extremely cold dry weather outside either: it is driving rain that drags them down.) Always leave the top door open unless there is a blizzard.

There should be clean fresh water in the stable; if not, make sure the pony can get to it every eight hours and eat damp food such as sugarbeet. If she wears a rug at night she must have a New Zealand rug when she is turned out during the day unless the weather is fine and warm. Bring her in at about 6 p.m. and give her a bulked-up feed and a haynet. Feed her again in the morning. If the stable opens into the field, give her a morning haynet in the stable and leave the door open; if not, you will have to give hay in the field.

If you are going to ride in the morning your plan should be: check water; give half a feed outside while you clean the stable; groom thoroughly; saddle and ride. This makes sure she has had enough time to digest after feeding, while the grooming will stimulate the circulation and wake her up. On returning turn her out with her remaining half feed and a haynet.

Constant Stabling

Constant stabling causes problems with boredom, digestion and circulation. Stabled ponies are liable to become irritable and too excitable when first out.

A stabled pony must go out, either ridden or free, for at least a couple of hours each day. A sick horse, unless she really cannot move, must also have a couple of short gentle strolls each day, for her circulation and digestion only work properly if she moves about. Otherwise her legs 'fill', that is, puff up, and she gets constipated easily.

The horse's digestion is not suited to eating two meals a day as ours is; the more feeds you can give the better. Four is a minimum. Work out how much must be in each to fulfil her daily ration (see chapter 8). She must not go without food for long periods. If this means she eats too much hay, feed whole or sliced turnips, which are mostly water but keep her amused. Having something to munch on wards off stable vices. A typical day will go:

6–7 a.m. *(before your breakfast)*   Check water; first feed, a little hay.
After breakfast   Muck out; knock over (i.e. groom lightly); exercise for at least one and a half hours.

12 noon   Feed; groom thoroughly and strap (this will take an hour altogether); hay.

2 p.m.   Turn out if possible.

6 p.m.   Check bed for the night; night rugs; feed; hay.

Bedtime   Feed.

As you can see, avoiding putting stress on your pony involves a good deal of strain on yourself, but it is the only way to ensure that a constantly stabled animal does not break down mentally and physically.

It is, as you can probably see, not realistic to keep a single pony permanently stabled if you are at work or at school. You would have to forgo one feed and shift the exercise period to early in the morning or late at night, which would get impossible in the winter. You could manage an in-and-out system, putting the pony out before work, and exercising and bringing him in when you get home.

If you have no land at all you should not plan on traditional stabling but instead use a covered yard or large open barn (see page 79) and keep the pony with a companion. He would then have the freedom to move, play and have some social life. You could feed two or three times daily, leaving hay always available, and ride at weekends or on fine evenings. The pony would stay moderately fit and would not suffer many of the stresses normally felt in confinement.

Caring for a Stabled Pony

You must provide the total diet of a stabled pony. Vitamins and minerals can be added as a supplement, of which there are many on the market. It is cheaper and better for the pony to give a mineral block and a good ration of mixed fresh vegetables; most greengrocers are happy to turn over their waste cabbage leaves and bruised fruit. The food should also contain wet sugarbeet pulp, which also wards off constipation. This naturally occurs if the pony only eats dry, concentrated food and is not able to move about enough.

It is said that routine is important to a stabled animal and that not sticking to a routine can cause colic. However, it appears to be more true to say that it is breaks in an otherwise strict routine that cause the trouble. More likely causes of colic, which is common in constantly stabled ponies but not in those kept outside, are feeding too much concentrated food, the stress of unnatural feeding, the general stress of being stabled and worms. In their natural environment ponies do not have meals that fill their bellies at special times; they never have empty bellies either. Setting up meal times means that you train the digestion to work at particular times only, and a meal that arrives early or late is not properly digested. Feeding little and often, and making sure the pony always has something to pick at, is a more natural system, and one that does not make the pony anxious. If you think he is eating his hay too fast, make a small-mesh haynet.

On days when the pony is liable to get less exercise, feed more hay and succulents or a beet mash and reduce the amount of concentrates. However, if you want to exercise him vigorously in the morning, feed him only a little hay beforehand and give him the rest when you get back, so he will not be leaping about on a full stomach.

Some stabled ponies eat their bedding, either because they are bored or because they do not get enough bulk feed. Outdoors, ponies spend about fifteen hours a day eating and stabled ponies also feel a constant urge to chew. There is nothing terrible about eating fresh, clean straw, although it may make some ponies cough, and with soiled straw self-infection from worms is an obvious hazard. Eating bedding is less likely on deep litter (see page 80). If it is a problem, provide more vegetables and hay, use a small-mesh haynet, turn the pony out as much as possible and bed on shredded paper, wood or shavings.

Care of the skin is very important for a stabled pony, particularly if she cannot roll. She should be groomed and strapped every day and encouraged to roll on the end of a lead rope after a ride. Rolling in a pile of sand in one corner of the yard is a delight for a stabled pony and relieves some of the strain of her unnatural life.

Ponies normally spend a good deal of their time touching and communicating with one another, so being forced to live in solitary confinement is another strain. Highly strung ponies, which unfortunately are usually the ones that are stabled, suffer most. Older stables have bars in the partitions so the animals can nuzzle each other, but in most modern stables this is not always possible. To relieve the strain of isolation, consider knocking out part of the partition and replacing it with a grille that can be removed once neighbouring ponies are friendly. An alternative is to remove the partitions and keep two or more ponies in the one box. It is not wise to put two strange ponies together in a stable; you will need to separate them with a chest-high bar for three weeks. Unless you are extremely unlucky and choose two ponies that take an instant dislike to each other, you will find that after this time they will be friends. Take care, though, to separate them when you give them their concentrates. Ponies that are good friends in the field can also be stabled together. If no other pony is available, you can provide a stable companion in the form of a goat, a sheep or a donkey.

Building Stables

If starting from scratch, design your stables so that you can alter the position of the partitions. This will enable you to keep ponies more as they would wish. Do not place the stables so that they face your exercise ground or a field in which other ponies are kept. Stabled animals tend to become agitated when they see other horses moving freely. Instead, try to arrange your stables so that they overlook a view where things are happening in the distance. This interests and soothes ponies; too much bustle close up excites them.

Make sure your stables have good ventilation; leaving open the top half of a stable door is not enough.

Yarding Ponies

In Eastern Europe and Russia, horses are yarded over winter like cattle, rather than being kept separately. The floor is covered in deep litter and the horses are tied up while being fed concentrates. Hay is given in racks. Covered yards are much better ventilated than ordinary stables and are more conducive to the animals' physical and mental health. If you are thinking of keeping a group of ponies together, it is well worth considering this method. Those pioneers who have tried it here find it works.

Bedding

Bedding should be deep or he will either not lie down or may bruise himself. Traditionally straw was always used for bedding; today peat, wood shavings and shredded paper are also used.

Deep litter

In a well-drained and well-ventilated stable the easiest and cheapest system is to build up a deep-litter bed. Start with a generous bed. Each morning for a week or more merely turn it so that droppings fall to the bottom and are covered. Remove anything soaking wet (most likely you will find this is always in the same place) but cover any damp patches with dry bedding. As time goes on add a little fresh bedding to cover dirt or damp. As the bed builds up you will find that the dirty layer at the bottom is heating up and absorbing any damp, like a manure heap but with a clean layer on top. Your pony thus has a thick warm mattress. Do not disturb the bed, but merely add fresh bedding, keeping your work and bedding bills to a minimum.

Building a good deep-litter bed does not mean neglect, but seeing that a natural process has a chance to establish itself. If the bed refuses to start drying out your floor may not be suitable or you may be disturbing it too much.

A good deep-litter bed will only use half to one bale of straw a week and lasts as long as you can still get in the stables.

Traditional mucking out

Remove all dung, dirty and wet bedding. Toss the rest lightly against the walls, leaving the centre of the floor to air. Replace the bed just before putting the horse in at night, adding fresh bedding daily. Reckon to use at least three bales of straw a week.

Building a good manure heap

Build your manure heap away from overhanging roofs and keep it square and straight-sided. Build up the edges first before filling in the middle. Tread down firmly every time you add fresh manure and keep the sides straight. A well-built manure heap rots down better than an untidy pile and can be sold to gardeners.

Righting a Cast Pony

When ponies roll in a box they sometimes get cast, that is, stuck with their legs folded against the wall so that they cannot roll back or get up. In this position they become frightened and are likely to panic. If you find your pony cast, calm him down and then go to find help. You will need two halters and lead ropes. With your helper, quietly thread the halters over the lower pair of legs, fitting them over knee and hock so that both joints will be cradled when you pull on the lead ropes. If he struggles, have your helper lean or sit on his neck just behind his head. When he realizes he cannot get up he will probably stop trying.

With both halters in place, stand behind the middle of his back, move both legs slightly in towards the middle of his body and then, using the lead ropes, pull steadily so that he rolls over towards you.

Figure 9 Righting a cast horse

After you have rolled him on to his back he will come over very fast, so be ready to spring back as four flailing feet come at you.

Never pull on the upper pair of legs or extend the front leg forwards or the rear one backwards, or you will tear his muscles. For your own safety do not try to roll a horse without ropes or get in amongst his legs.

With practice you can roll a horse single-handed with one good rope, but do not attempt it at first. If you have to wait for help, the pony will feel better if you sit quietly where he can see you and pretend everything is quite normal rather than fussing over him. Being floored and helpless terrifies ponies.

11 Tack and Riding Clothes

The Bridle

A simple bridle consists of two cheekpieces, a headpiece with throatlatch, a browband, a bit and a pair of reins. Bridles vary greatly in price depending on the quality of the leather. Good leather is thick, supple and does not stretch when pulled; poor leather stretches and snaps easily. It is better to buy a good, well-cared-for secondhand English bridle, or a webbing one, than a poor-quality new one. Cheap bridles tend to break at exactly the moments you need them most.

Bridle sizes are usually given as small pony, pony, cob and hunter. When buying at a sale, measure your pony's head with a tape

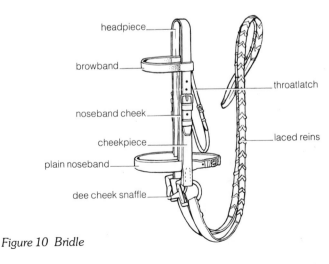

Figure 10 Bridle

measure from just above the corner of the mouth across the top of his head and down the other side. Check this measurement against the length of the bridle plus the bit rings.

Secondhand leather should be supple and uncracked. When inspecting a secondhand bridle, undo the buckles on the reins and cheekpieces and check the leather for signs of wear and dryness; these are the parts that break most often. Bend the leather to test it.

A noseband is not necessary but can have two uses: an ordinary noseband anchors a standing martingale, while a drop, a flash or a Grakle noseband keeps the pony's mouth shut. A well-behaved pony does not need a noseband, although, oddly enough, he will be thought undressed without one in the show ring.

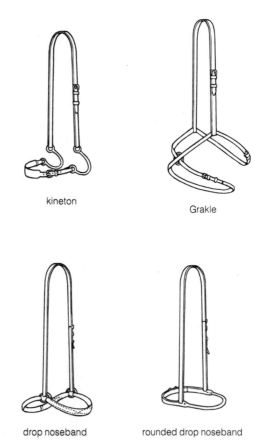

kineton

Grakle

drop noseband   rounded drop noseband

Figure 11 Special nosebands

Reins can be plain, rubber-covered (heavy, but easy to hold when wet), plaited or webbing. Webbing reins are washable and never break except at the leather ends, but some types can be harsh on young fingers.

The bridle should fit so that the bit is snug in the corners of the mouth, not dragging them up into a hideous grimace or hanging loose. A pony will tend to hold a loose bit in place with his tongue, so open his mouth to check he is not doing this. The throatlatch should be fastened so that there is room for three fingers to be slotted sideways between it and the pony's jaw. An ordinary noseband should have two fingers' width of room in it. The reins should be long enough to lie over the pommel of the saddle without being tight. If they are too long they will be a nuisance. The browband keeps the bridle from slipping backwards down the pony's neck. It must not be tight or it will irritate the pony and may cause head-shaking. You should be able to slip a couple of fingers inside it.

The Bit

The bit can mean confidence or misery to your pony. Of all your tack, it is the one piece you should not hesitate to be extravagant about. A good bit lasts a lifetime. Buy the best quality you can find, even if it means making do with a secondhand bridle or rope reins. A pony cares nothing for smartness, but she will resent an uncomfortable bit.

Finding the bit that suits your pony best is occasionally difficult, especially if the pony has had bad experiences. On the whole the kinder the bit the more likely the pony is to respond, which is the opposite of what most people assume. A pony that habitually pulls against the bit, jerks her nose up in the air, rears or appears to behave stupidly with her head is probably protesting about the pressure on her mouth. This may be because your hands are too heavy and rough or because the bit is too harsh, but most likely it is a combination of the two. Using a harsher bit in an attempt to 'control' the pony more will probably make matters worse, although some old, hard-mouthed ponies simply will not stop unless a fairly hard bit is used.

To find out if your pony would appreciate a lighter bit, try sewing a good layer of towelling round a metal bit, or borrow a selection of bits and try each for a week at a time. If you cannot stop your pony, do not immediately try a harder bit: learn to use your weight and seat better (see chapter 18).

Basically there are two types of bit, with hundreds of variations, and one well-known type of bitless bridle. These are the snaffle, the curb, and the hackamore.

The snaffle

A snaffle is almost always used in English riding. It is generally a jointed bit with rings. It acts on the bars or gums as well as the corners of the mouth and tends to raise the pony's head. The fatter the bit the kinder the action and the more likely the pony to cooperate.

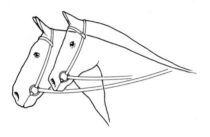

Figure 12 Snaffle bit in action. When pressure is put on the rein the pony's head is raised

The kindest bit of all, and one that should always be used on a young or soft-mouthed pony, is a flexible rubber bar without a joint. A curved vulcanite (light plastic) bar is also gentle in action.

An eggbutt snaffle is fixed on its rings and will not pinch the corners of the mouth; the fatter it is near the rings the softer it is on the mouth. An excellent bit is the German hollow-mouth eggbutt. Made of hollow stainless steel, it is virtually unbreakable, light and kind. A rubber-covered D-ring snaffle is also kind.

Thinner snaffles with upright bars or rubber shields just inside the rings are harder in action but still protect the corners of the mouth. They are often useful for determined old ponies ridden by small children. The traditional thinner English snaffles are not particularly soft: they have a nutcracker action on the corners of the mouth and if used harshly the joint presses into the roof of the mouth, making the pony raise his head. Cheap thin snaffles should be thrown away. Gag snaffles are harsh and should not be used by novices.

86

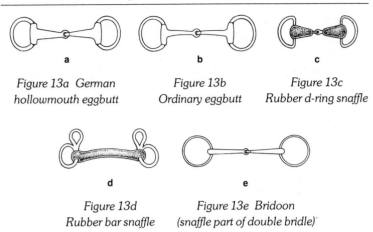

Figure 13a German
hollowmouth eggbutt

Figure 13b
Ordinary eggbutt

Figure 13c
Rubber d-ring snaffle

Figure 13d
Rubber bar snaffle

Figure 13e Bridoon
(snaffle part of double bridle)

There are other older snaffles, twisted or double, with a host of other devices to make the bit harsher. These were used on big, hard-mouthed horses, often ones whose mouths had been ruined by driving or hunting with the old-fashioned seat: they have little place in modern riding.

The curb
A curb has a straight or curved bar with shanks at the sides and a chain or strap going round the pony's chin. It puts pressure on the chin, on the bars of the mouth, and on the poll, and tends to lower the pony's head. A curb has much more stopping power than a snaffle.

A curb bit is fitted so that it does not quite wrinkle the corners of the mouth; the chain is twisted until it lies flat before being fastened with a hook. The longer the shank, the tighter the chain, or the harder the chain, the more severe the action. A long-shanked curb puts a great deal of pressure on the horse and so takes a good deal of skill to use.

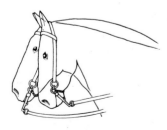

Figure 14 Curb bit in action

A pure curb is hardly ever seen in Britain but is used in Western and Spanish riding. However, it is a mistake to think that this is cruel, for the style of riding is quite different. The horse is ridden on a loose rein and responds to a neck-rein and the rider's weight. The bit is rarely used but is there to remind the horse to respond to those gentle suggestions. Riding badly on a snaffle is far crueller than riding well on a curb.

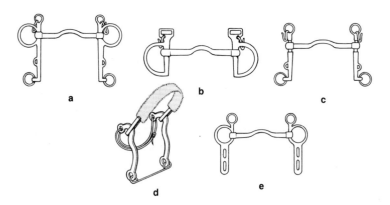

Figure 15a Pelham, b Kimblewick, c Slide cheek Weymouth with port – the curb bit of a double bridle, d Western type hackamore, e Liverpool

The curb most often used in Britain is the Pelham, which has two reins: the upper uses the bit on the bars, and the lower uses the curb. It is quite difficult to manage the two reins well in ordinary hacking or hunting, and if a Pelham is being used on a pony that is hard to stop the upper and lower rein rings are often connected together with a leather rounder so that only one rein is used. This means the curb action is very mild, and as a straight bit is itself gentler than a jointed one, the result is often pleasing.

The Kimblewick has a D in place of the two rings and joiner. By all bitting theory it is a nonsensical bit, yet a surprising number of ponies go well in it. There are two possible positions for the single rein: one gives more snaffle action and one more curb.

A Liverpool bit is a curb bit with slots down the shank so that the leverage on the curb can be altered. It is used for driving, but can be an interesting bit to experiment with as you can see if your pony goes better in a straight bar (rein level with bit, without a chain), a Kimblewick-type action or a true curb or Pelham.

The double bridle

A double bridle has two bits, a snaffle (called a bridoon) and a curb, each with a separate rein. It is used for precise control of the head position and is difficult to use correctly, needing good hands. It is most often seen in the show ring (often, alas, used badly) and in dressage.

Holding double reins

The two reins can be held in different ways, according to which authority you follow; each swears his own way is 'correct'. Usually both reins are threaded through the hand separated by the ring, or ring and little, fingers. It has become fashionable to have the curb rein uppermost, although it seems more logical, as well as giving more variable control on the curb, to have the reins the other way up.

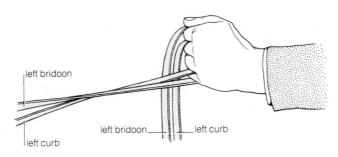

left bridoon

left bridoon   left curb

left curb

Figure 16 Holding double reins

Size of bit

Bits are measured in inches across the mouthpiece. It is important that a bit fits properly: if too small or too large it will rub. If you do not know what size to buy, borrow several different sized ones and try them until you find the right one.

An unusual sight nowadays: the little girl (then Princess Elizabeth) rides with double reins while out hacking with her father. Notice the reins are not crossed

Hackamores and bitless bridles

A hackamore has a curb but no bit, the curb acting off the noseband. Again, the longer the shank the more powerful the action. A long-shanked English hackamore is very powerful since it acts on the poll as well as closing round the nose. Western hackamores do not usually act on the poll.

90

A hackamore should be fitted so the noseband comes about two fingers' breadth below the cheekbone. Too low a hackamore can break the end of the nasal bones if pulled hard.

A hackamore is meant to be used Western-style: that is, you should use the neck-rein and your weight more than in normal English riding and ride on a loose rein without any contact. Pulling one rein will not turn the pony.

Hackamores are particularly useful for Arab ponies, which tend to dislike bits and to like being ridden with weight and legs alone, and for other ponies which hate or ignore a bit (see photographs on pages 172–3).

Gentle or young ponies, again particularly the Arab sort, can often be ridden off a padded noseband alone. If more pressure is needed for stopping, a bridle can be made up to give a gentle curb action.

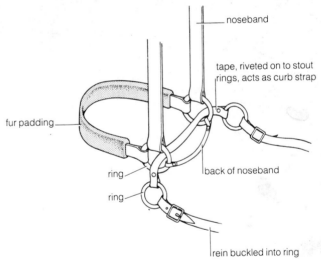

Figure 17 Homemade bitless bridle with light curb action

Martingales

A standing martingale is fixed to an ordinary noseband to stop a pony chucking his head up or sticking his nose out too far; it sometimes stops rearing. It should be fitted so that it is loose when the pony's head is in a reasonable position and only tightens when he misbehaves. Never jump in a standing martingale.

Grakle noseband, jointed snaffle with cheekpieces (Fillis snaffle) and running martingale. This combination is used on this fit, determined pony because she tends to evade the bit by sticking her head in the air and crossing her jaw. The Grakle makes her yield to the bit and the running martingale stops her star-gazing. Another solution might be to use a Pelham.

The rider seems to be putting a good deal of pressure on the rein despite the fact that the pony is standing still with someone in front of her. This is a skewbald pony

A running martingale runs on two rings fitted on the reins and is used to make sure that the pull on the reins is in the right direction, i.e. horizontal, or downwards if the pony's head is far too high. It is useful when the pony consistently carries his head too high, as for example with an excitable jumping pony or when the rider is not good enough to correct this tendency.

Unfortunately many novices regard a running martingale as a smart fashion and an excuse not to improve their standard of riding. It is often a sign that a rider has rough, badly placed hands and would be better suited to a quieter pony.

The Saddle

Saddles are expensive and an ill-fitting saddle is worse than useless. A well-cared-for secondhand saddle is often a better buy than a new one of poorer quality.

Saddles are measured in inches from the stud on the side of the pommel to the back of the cantle. This gives the length of the seat but not the width, which is just as important to the pony, so when buying you may be better off describing the height of the pony and whether he has low, high, wide or narrow withers. Try to arrange to see the saddle on the pony, without a numnah, before you buy. A correctly fitting saddle sits at the right angle with someone on it. From the back you should see that there is a column of air all the way along the pony's spine. There must be room to slot all your fingers between the withers and the pommel, even when the rider rocks forward. This is extremely important as any pressure on the withers causes irritation and even a fistula (see chapter 26). The saddle must not be so narrow that it digs into the side of the withers either. If the pony is unusually fat or thin you will have to make allowances for changes. All this means that buying a saddle does have pitfalls, and a novice would be better to take expert advice.

Saddles have different cuts. The modern general-purpose saddle generally has a deeper seat than the older, flatter hunting or polo saddle. Most have kneerolls, and in some these may be so pronounced that they literally hold you into one position. While this looks comfortable and gives security in fast cross-country work like eventing, such a saddle is not suitable for the novice as it encourages too short a stirrup and does not allow the rider to develop a secure seat on his own. A medium-cut saddle is far more comfortable if you intend to spend long hours in it.

Jumping saddles have forward-cut flaps to suit the shorter stirrups used, and are cut back at the withers. Dressage saddles are very straight, with a deep seat, while racing saddles are tiny, with extremely forward-cut flaps.

Cavalry saddles are seldom found but are excellent for adults riding ponies as they encourage a good seat and distribute the weight better than do normal saddles. Western saddles are expensive and heavy but again distribute weight better than English saddles. Again there

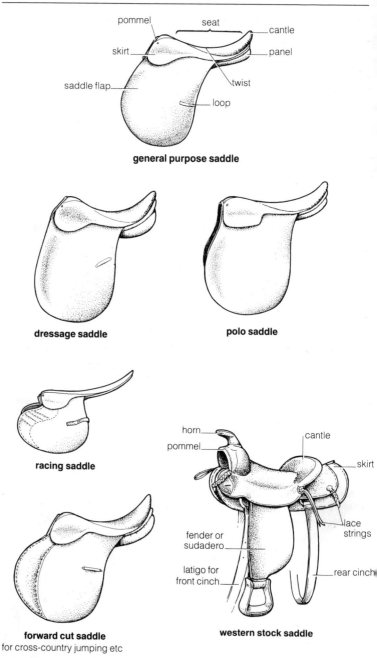

general purpose saddle

dressage saddle

polo saddle

racing saddle

forward cut saddle
for cross-country jumping etc

western stock saddle

Figure 18 Saddles

94

are differences in cut. A Western saddle must not be used without a good blanket.

Beware of Indian and Pakistani saddles. Far cheaper than their English counterparts, they are made of good-quality leather but have poor trees, so that if used a lot they tend to collapse and cause sores. Moreover, they tend to be cut so curiously that they fit no pony properly.

When buying a secondhand saddle check carefully that the tree, the framework on which the leatherwork rests, is sound. Brace the cantle against your stomach and grasp each side of the pommel. Pull the pommel towards the cantle. If the saddle gives, the tree is broken in the seat. Spring-tree saddles do give a little, but if you test one or two new saddles you will get the feel of how much is permissible. Secondly, pull your hands apart to test the arch in the pommel. There should be no movement at all. If you feel a slight movement check that the arch has not come out of the pockets at the front. These can be mended but a broken arch cannot. A saddle with a broken tree is worthless. Check also that there are three girth pulls and that they are not worn. The padding under the seat should not be too flattened with use (again, compare a new saddle). It is possible to have a saddle restuffed but it is a fairly major job; replacing girth pulls is relatively easy.

Stirrups

Stirrup irons should be a good ½-inch wider than the widest part of the foot. Stainless-steel irons are far superior to nickel ones, which can break suddenly. Some stirrups have offset eyes so that they hang crooked on the leathers. They should hang so the higher side is at the front when the stirrup lies flat, that is, on the outside of the rider's foot. Rubber footrests provide a firmer grip, especially to smooth rubber soles.

Stirrup leathers should be checked regularly for wear.

Girths

The modern padded girth is far the best. It is easily washed and unlikely to rub. Girth galls, friction sores caused by dirty or harsh girths, are difficult to get rid of, as well as being extremely irritating to the pony, so it is worth paying a little more for a good girth. Lampwick girths are also kind; string girths do rub unless kept meticulously clean; leather girths are expensive and very good if well cared for, but if allowed to dry out they will rub and break suddenly.

If your pony is thin-skinned or irritable about having the girth done up, buy or make a girth cover of several layers of artificial fur. This is soft, comfortable and easy to wash.

Numnah

A numnah is a sheepskin, artificial fur or quilted pad that goes under the saddle. It keeps the pony's back dry and the saddle free from sweat. A badly placed numnah can cause sore withers. When saddling up, always pull the numnah up into the pommel, ensuring that there is air between the numnah and the withers and that the blood flow is not restricted.

Blanket

A thick folded blanket can be used instead of a numnah. A blanket can also be used if the pony has lost a lot of weight and the saddle threatens to rub on the withers. Fold the blanket into a rectangle some 6 inches wider than needed and turn over the front to make a double-thickness band along the front edge. Make sure the blanket is pulled up into the pommel and is not tight over the withers.

Crupper

A crupper runs from the back of the saddle to the tail to stop the saddle slipping forward. It is extremely valuable on small round ponies with low withers and is essential on a donkey. The saddle must be fitted with a ring at the back.

Breastband

A breastband stops the saddle slipping back, a less frequent problem with ponies.

Harness

Working harness

'Work' here means hauling logs, a harrow, plough, or anything else that will stop of its own accord. The pony is often led rather than driven. The harness consists of a collar and hames or a breastplate; a pad which goes over the pony's back and usually does not fasten underneath; and a pair of chains.

The collar should fit to give three fingers' clearance under the neck when the load is applied. Some collars can be unbuckled at the top, but if not they must go over the pony's head upside-down and be turned over on the neck. The hames are metal bracers that fit over the collar and carry the chains or traces. Chains are usually used for field work as they do not break or burn like ropes do. They pass through loops on the pad before going to the load.

A breastplate cannot be used for heavy and prolonged work but is adequate for pulling, say, a sledge. Care should be taken to see that it does not ride too high and choke the pony. Usually a string or strap over the neck holds it in place.

When first using a breastplate or collar, check carefully for signs of irritation of the skin and pad accordingly.

Horses in working harness: this is the best harness for a ploughing match

Driving harness

There are many different types of driving harness, from the lightest fashionable gear to heavy farm tack. When buying and fitting always remember that a trap must be (a) pulled, (b) carried and (c) braked, and you will be able to sort out and fit any harness safely.

In the lightest types of harness pulling is done by a breastband via traces that attach to the front of the trap; carrying by passing the shafts of the trap through tugs, loops strapped to the sides of the pad, which fastens under the pony; and braking by small pegs on the shafts that brace against the tugs from behind (there may also be a brake on the trap).

In a standard driving harness pulling is done by collar, hames and traces; carrying by tugs and braking by breeching, a harness that attaches to the back of the pad and fits round the pony's rump; it is then hooked to the shafts so that as the weight of the trap comes forward it is braced against the pony's rump.

In heavy farm-cart harness pulling is done by collar and hames that attach via short chains directly to the shafts, there being no traces; carrying by a heavy chain that runs over metal grooves in a heavy pad

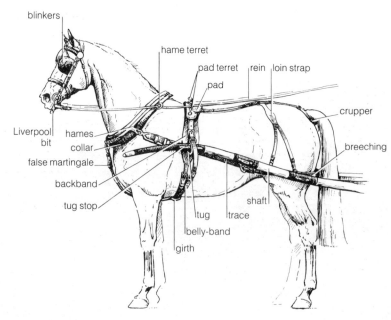

Figure 19 Standard driving harness

to a second pair of hooks on the shafts; and braking by breeching that attaches to a third pair of hooks. On a two-wheel cart there is also a bellyband that stops the shafts flying up in the air.

It is evident, then, that different pieces of different harnesses will not necessarily be interchangeable and that you must check to see that the harness suits the trap as well as the pony.

Care of Tack

Dirty and stiff leather causes chafing and sores that are difficult to cure unless the pony is left unworked; it also breaks easily. Leather is cleaned with oil or soap.

For oil use neatsfoot or a proprietary brand. Linseed and other oils are not suitable. Oils, neatsfoot especially, soften, darken and water-proof leather. Tack that has been consistently well oiled is almost black, completely pliable, and unharmed by water. Neatsfoot is the best softener of old, neglected leather and the best cleaning stuff for everyday tack. Simply wipe off mud and dirt with a damp sponge and apply oil with another sponge or a brush.

Saddle soap (glycerine soap) does not soften or darken leather to the same extent as oil does. It is more suitable for tack you wish to keep looking like new. Wipe off any sweat with a damp sponge, wash the sponge well, then work the soap into a good lather before applying it to the leather. Once it is dry you can work up a dull sheen with a soft cloth, but riding tack is never shiny.

Clean tack every half dozen times you use it. If it is wet, leave it to dry (but *not* near a heat source) and then oil or soap it well, working the leather until suppleness returns. Undo every buckle and pay special attention to folds in the leather, where it tends to dry out and crack.

Leather should not be kept in a centrally heated house: it dries out. Store tack in a cool dry place.

Polish a bit with a soft cloth but *not* with metal polish.

Riding Clothes

It is foolish to ride without a proper hat of approved standard. Many older hats do not meet European safety standards; those that do are marked. A good hat is expensive but you cannot afford to economize. Children are often careless about doing up the chin strap, which is equally foolish.

If you ride a lot you will find jodhpurs far more comfortable than trousers or jeans, for they have a patch on the inside of the knee so you do not get rubbed by the seam or nipped by the stirrup leathers. Stretch jodhpurs are smart and some are almost indistinguishable from ordinary stretch jeans. White or cream ones are usually worn when competing but are rather impractical for everyday use.

Elastic-sided jodhpur boots are comfortable and practical; they are also worn by children when showing. Long leather riding boots are expensive; cheap rubber versions look the same but are cold in winter. Wellington boots are too clumsy for riding and can get stuck in the stirrup if you fall off. If you have no proper riding boots, for everyday riding use flat boots or shoes that will slip easily out of the stirrup.

A proper hacking jacket is also comfortable. Dark ones are worn when showing. Never ride in a crackly plastic jacket or anorak: most ponies hate the noise of them and in a wind you may find yourself charging off out of control.

Riding in the rain is more enjoyable than it might seem provided you are well waterproofed. Long riding macs strap round the legs and are slit up the back so you sit comfortably. Waterproof trousers will ride up your leg unless you put elastic under the soles of your feet. Gloves usually slip on wet leather reins. Rubber, webbing or plaited string reins are safer.

12 Worming, Care of the Feet and Shoeing, Inoculations

Worming

Ponies should be routinely wormed at least every six months, even if the pasture is changed and the risk of reinfection low. If the risk of reinfestation is greater, worm up to every six to eight weeks. When moving a pony to new pasture, worm two days beforehand. The day after worming, check the fresh dung carefully for traces of worms.

Roundworms

Three types of roundworm, a tapeworm, lungworm and bots all affect ponies. They produce similar symptoms: general unthriftiness, lack of energy, harsh, staring coat, a fat belly but thin back and haunches. Ponies with pinworm often scratch their tails (but so do ponies with lice). Severe redworm can cause anaemia, turning the inside of the lower eyelid white, rather than a healthy pale pink.

Redworms are about ½ inch long, red and coiled; they are not easy to see. If they are visible in the dung the pony should be rewormed every six weeks until they are eradicated. Redworm cause a great deal of damage to the pony by burrowing through the gut wall; immature redworm are a frequent cause of colic. Pasture that is known to be infested with redworm should be well limed, rested, and if possible not used by ponies for a couple of years.

Pin, thread or maw worms are about the size and colour of a matchstick, thinner at one end. They do not cause the pony much distress unless very numerous, when the pony will scratch her tail, due to the female worms laying eggs round the anus.

Large roundworm (ascarids) are up to a foot long, smooth and

101

eel-like, and often come away with the dung. Some wormers recommend a higher dose rate against large roundworm.

Tapeworm
Tapeworm does not occur frequently in horses and is difficult to detect.

Lungworm
Lungworm is caught from donkeys and causes coughing and unthriftiness.

Bots
Bots are the immature larvae of the gadfly (see chapter 26).

If a pony needs worming frequently it is good practice to change the wormer regularly. The easiest, most effective but most expensive wormers come in a syringe whose contents you inject into the pony's mouth. If you squirt the paste over the pony's back teeth you can be fairly certain he will take it all in. Cheaper are powders which are mixed in with food. They are said to be tasteless but some canny ponies do taste and refuse them or, maddeningly, only eat half the dosed feed. If you have difficulty with both paste and powder, try mixing a powder with treacle and feed it in a sandwich.

Ivermectin is the only wormer which eradicates lungworm and bots as well as stomach worms.

The Feet and Shoeing

Ponies' feet evolved without shoes and an unshod foot, unless either overworked so that it is worn or kept on soft ground where it does not wear down, is healthier than a shod one. In the unshod foot the central spongy frog hits the ground before the rest of the foot (that is its function), cushioning the foot and leg from jarring and preventing the lower leg from being concussed. It also acts as a pump to keep the blood circulating within the foot. In a shod foot the frog does not touch the ground and tends to reduce gradually in size. As a result, the bones of the leg suffer concussion. Hence it is important not to shoe a pony before he is four if possible, lest his young bones are jarred while still growing.

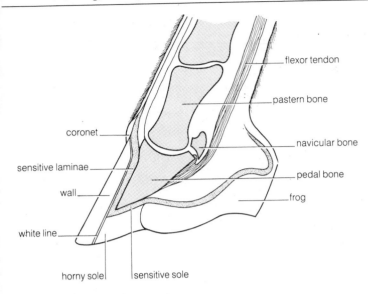

Figure 20 Structure of foot

Arabs, Welsh Mountain, Exmoor and some other native ponies have excellent hard feet with arched soles that are not easily bruised. If your pony has these good feet, if you do not ride every day and you ride mostly on grass, you may not have to shoe her. You will have to make sure you ride less than two or three miles a week on the road, that you never go faster than a walk on tarmac or stony tracks, and that you use every scrap of grass verge (you will find that the pony does this for you after a while). If the pony becomes tender-footed you are overdoing work on hard ground. Tarmac files the hoof short so it bruises easily.

Pay special attention to the outer rim of an unshod pony's hoof. Just inside the edge there is a white line of softer horn in which small stones may get stuck. They will make the pony very sore and if left may work their way up inside the hoof, causing lameness for days or weeks until they burst out in an abscess (quittor) on the coronet. If you find that small stones have caused a hole in the white line, pick them out, clean the hole and pack it tightly with shredded bale string (the hemp sort) soaked in Stockholm tar.

If the pony does not put down his feet evenly they will become misshapen after a while and need trimming. Be sure to ask the

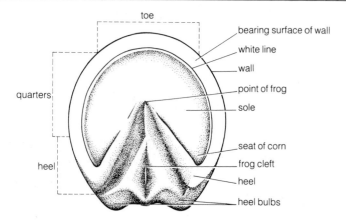

Figure 21 Foot from underneath

blacksmith to take off as little as possible from the sole and frog, explaining that you ride the pony unshod.

Many children find that they can ride so little in the winter that their ponies only need shoeing in spring and summer. However, if a pony is left unridden for long periods and is kept on soft land, she will need the farrier every two months or so or her feet will grow too long. Overlong feet are liable to split and tear; they put great strain on the tendons, which will cause serious damage if the pony is ridden occasionally and the growing horn forms at the wrong angle, so the foot gradually deteriorates.

Shoes

Most ponies in regular use will need shoeing every six to eight weeks whether the shoes are worn out or not, for the growth of the foot means that the shoes no longer fit. Ask your local pony club or riding school about a good blacksmith. Farriers must now be properly qualified and bad shoeing is less common than it used to be, but some are more patient than others, some more used to remedial work, and so on. If your pony is nervous about his feet you should choose your farrier carefully.

If you cannot get your pony to the forge, arrange to meet your farrier somewhere where he can work under cover if it rains, on a clean hard surface and in good light. Shoes can be put on hot or cold.

104

The blacksmith's visit: clenching down the nails on a newly shod foot. From right to left note: the farrier's box of tools, the tripod on which he rests the horse's foot, the anvil (behind the horse's belly), the gas cylinder, tube and heater for the portable forge. There is also a bucket of water for cooling the shoe. The handler holds the horse loosely so he can see what the farrier is doing.

This excellent Welsh cob stallion (note the good head, well-shaped neck, laid-back shoulder, short strong back and splendid legs) is in poor condition, having run out with a herd of mares on the mountain until autumn. He will now be stabled, fed well and exercised over winter

If heated they tend to stay on better, but some farriers cold-shoe very efficiently. Nowadays most farriers buy ready-made shoes, heat them in a portable forge, and shape them while hot to fit the pony's feet.

When phoning to make an appointment, give the pony's shoe size measured from side to side at the widest point; if he is unshod

105

measure the foot. Give a week's notice; you may need more in summer. Farriers can seldom guarantee to be punctual but you must be ready on time, with the pony's feet clean, a handful or two of food to keep him amused, and a bucket of cold water for quenching the hot shoes.

Treat your farrier with courtesy and you will learn a great deal from him. Farriers are highly trained and the older ones have often tended the same horses for years, gaining great experience. You may find yourself consulting your farrier before your vet on many queries. This being so, most farriers do not appreciate criticism from amateurs who think they know more than they do. Nevertheless, there are some points you can check to see your pony is well shod.

First, the shoe should be shaped to fit the foot rather than the other way round. This is easier said than seen, for the farrier will trim and shape the foot before shoeing. The coronet should be parallel to the ground so that the foot is level. The front of the hoof should continue the line of the pastern, that is, at about 50° in front, 55° behind. The back of the hoof should be parallel to the front. An undershot or weak heel can cause serious foot problems; a good blacksmith will stimulate growth by using long-heeled shoes.

The vast majority of ponies are perfectly straightforward to shoe, but in some cases, for instance if the pony has had severe laminitis, has badly shaped feet or moves badly, special shoes may have to be made.

If the pony goes lame within a day or two of being shod, call the farrier again. It is possible he may have driven a nail too close to the quick and pricked the pony, especially if the pony objected while being shod. In this case the nail will have to be replaced.

Do not leave the shoes on too long. As the foot grows the toe carries the shoe forward so the back corners are no longer on the heels but on the seat of corn, which causes soreness and even an abscess. Leaving shoes on too long also causes stressed tendons and joints, stumbling, overreaching and an unhealthy foot.

When shoes are worn from roadwork they get loose; you can hear a tinkling as one foot goes down. They can be tightened temporarily by hammering down the clenches, that is, the part of the nail above the foot. Hammer the nails in tight from underneath, put the pony's foot down and tap the clenches down to take up the slack on the nail. This is not as easy as it sounds.

Growth rings caused by change of diet. The rings only appear about halfway down the foot, that is, about six months ago. This foot is overgrown and needs reshoeing. This, and the similarity of the rings to those caused by laminitis, means that the foot should be carefully inspected underneath. If the pony has had laminitis the frog will be poor and the sole flat and oval in shape, reaching right to the front of the foot so that there is no room for further trimming. If, as in this case, the foot is normal but overgrown, the sole will be round and raised off the ground by the overgrown wall, while the shoe will be carried forward on the foot by the extra growth

If you are going to leave the pony unridden, have the shoes taken off first or they will tear off when the feet are overgrown and may cause serious damage. If you leave the pony unshod for winter, have his toes rounded off after the shoes come off, or they will chip and split.

Inoculations

Ponies can be inoculated against tetanus (lockjaw) and flu (equine influenza). Usually both are combined in a single injection given once a year. This gives protection against several strains of flu.

However, it seems that the injection affects some ponies badly, and that in some it may spark off COPD (see page 215). Try to balance this risk against that of your pony catching flu, which will vary with district and how you use the pony. As flu is infectious, a pony that does not often meet strangers is unlikely to catch it; a show pony or one at livery in a dealer's yard is more at risk. Some shows demand that all competing ponies are vaccinated.

Tetanus is commonly picked up from a deep puncture wound, and is usually fatal. If your pony has not been vaccinated against it, and gets such a wound, be sure to have the vet give an anti-tetanus injection immediately.

Insurance

You can insure your pony against death, loss of use and vet's bills. As with other insurance, terms vary so check the small print carefully.

Freeze-branding

The high price of horsemeat means that rustling is a problem in some areas. Stolen ponies are usually slaughtered immediately, but a branded pony, being instantly identifiable, is generally abandoned: the largest freeze-branding firm reports a 100 per cent recovery rate. Freeze-branding is done by applying a supercooled iron. It is quick and humane and is done by the firm's operator, not the vet. Check horse magazines for advertisements.

13 Getting on with Your Pony

If you are to handle your pony well you must appreciate that his view of the world is completely different from yours and that what is obvious and desirable to you is not necessarily so to him. Ponies do not care about winning cups and rosettes, or about being clean or impressing the neighbours; they do care about friendliness, amusement and food, and about feeling safe from attack. It is easier for you to understand her point of view than make her understand yours, but if she trusts you she will be happy to go along with your schemes.

Ponies are natural followers, choosing bold and trustworthy leaders. During early training the young pony, which is nervous since she is undergoing many new experiences, learns to trust people as she trusts older ponies. A good trainer is quiet, confident, consistent, and never makes mistakes. It is not a question of teaching the pony who is master but of earning his respect. It is up to you as his later owner to earn his respect too. This means you must always be calm, certain and trustworthy, for a pony will not follow a dithery or foolish person any more than you would; in fact, he will try to get away from one. The thing you have to master is your fear and uncertainty, not your horse.

It is understandable that a person should be nervous of animals as large as ponies, but anyone who spends enough time watching them realizes their gentle nature. They loaf or graze quietly together; every now and then they scratch each other's necks for a few minutes; they like to be lazy and comfortable. Unlike dogs, they have no interest for chasing, biting and worrying; we really would have something to fear if they did. Ponies seldom squabble and when they do it is usually about food in containers or being closed in together. Both of these are conditions of our making. On the whole ponies prefer to walk away from arguments.

If you are nervous about your pony at first, spend a good deal of time around her. Weed the field around her; take her out for a graze, sitting quietly a few yards away while she eats. Do not feel you have to be doing things to her; simply aim to spend a few hours a day in her company so you can both learn to relax together. As you get used to her behaviour you will realize that actions you might have thought were aimed nastily at you are ones that she would do anyway. She stamps a hind foot to get rid of flies, not necessarily to kick you; she scratches on posts and trees even when you are not riding her; she turns quickly to face sudden sounds, not to unseat you. Being large and gentle, ponies do not realize how fragile people feel about themselves; they are apt to treat us like other ponies, which sometimes alarms us.

Learn to interpret your pony's body movements and signals just as other ponies do. When startled, a pony raises his head and tail and moves jerkily. Others in the herd, seeing this, know he thinks something is wrong. If you are by nature a quick, jerky person you will have to learn to slow your movements or ponies will misunderstand you, thinking you have spotted a tiger. Learn to move in a calm, unhurried way, with your shoulders and arms relaxed, and do not allow yourself to become overexcited even when you think disaster is about to strike.

Tension in a pony is shown in the neck and mouth, both of which become tight. Watch his eyes and ears carefully and you will see what is causing the worry. An irritated pony wriggles his skin, lashes his tail gently or wrinkles his nostrils. A frightened pony tends to pull back with eyes and ears rolled back. A pony that is relaxing after worry has passed makes small munching movements with his mouth. Learn to watch these signs and to read your pony's body language. Ponies expect us to understand this language, which is perfectly plain to them and which they use when they are trying to tell us something.

When you start working with your pony, be calm, certain and determined. Do not shout at your pony or jerk away if he objects to what you are doing. Often when you are uncertain yourself your lack of confidence is interpreted by the pony as a sign that there is something suspicious about your intentions. Ponies do not take advantage of beginners so much as dislike and mistrust behaviour they think is sinister. For instance, you may want to pick up a pony's foot but feel nervous about it. When you run your hand down her leg, trembling, she of course snatches her foot away. There are three things you might do. First, you might jump back in alarm, then try again even more cautiously and then give up. As a result, you tell yourself you can't do it and the pony tells herself she was quite right to suspect you. Second, you might hit the pony to 'make her behave'. Depending on the character of the pony, she might utterly refuse to behave or she might stand obediently this time. However, the chances are that on the whole she will gradually come to dislike you more and more until she refuses to do anything for you, especially be caught. Third, you can simply take no notice of the pony's fuss and run your hand down her leg again immediately. Probably the pony will increase her fuss for a couple more tries, but she will suddenly sigh and allow you to pick up her foot, whereupon you can praise her. The next time it will go more easily, and so on. This slow persistence, the refusal to be turned from your aim, is the kind of firmness that works with ponies. Unfortunately too many people think that firmness means a good slap on the bottom, which may work once but in the end produces a pony that takes no pleasure in being with you.

Praise your pony when she has done something well, especially if she is learning. Do not, however, make the mistake of telling her she is a good girl before she has done anything at all, or your words and praise have no meaning. Immediately she has done something 'good', speak warmly to her and rub her neck. Too many people are quick to be angry when a pony has done something 'wrong', but often the animal is not sure what is being asked or knows that if he does it he will only be asked again and again (especially jumping). Ponies will not work for punishment any more than we will, and they like praise as much as we do. Make much of your pony; he is not a machine.

If you watch ponies together you will see that their friendship is expressed in being together and in grooming each other occasionally. They do not give one another titbits and croon soppily over one another. Copy them. Give a pony a treat when you catch him, when you release him, and maybe when he is learning something new, but do not always be giving him treats without reason or you will make him silly and bad-tempered.

111

When you meet different ponies you will notice that some are spoilt, some sweet-tempered, some full of interest and others half asleep. Of course ponies do vary in character, but these differences are more a reflection of the way they are handled. Watch carefully and you will see the difference in owners. You will see also how a pony may change dramatically after a year or two with a new owner. Take note of what the better people do and copy them. Do not be fooled into admiring someone who is 'managing' a difficult pony. The true sign of excellence is to have a pony that is not difficult to handle. Do not be afraid to ask advice of the good horsemen. These people are good because they are always trying to improve themselves and they are almost invariably humble about their own excellence. They will not scorn your ignorance but will admire and sympathize with your willingness to learn.

14 Handling and Tacking Up

Ponies do not like people who shout, wave their hands about, get flustered, and get into flaps and rages.

Handling

Catching

When catching a pony in the field, take a treat and put the halter over your shoulder so that he sees the pleasure rather than the work ahead. If he does not come when you call, walk towards him, approaching slightly at an angle so he can see you properly. If he walks away, keep walking to one side of him, but do not run or grab at him or he will feel attacked and run away. When he stands, give him the titbit and put one hand on his neck. Slide your arm over his neck, standing close beside him with one hip just in front of his shoulders. Ponies are usually caught from the left, so it is your right arm that goes over his neck. Slip the halter off your shoulder and put it round his nose with your left hand, pulling it up over his ears with your right. If you are using a headcollar do not flip the strap annoyingly over his poll. Pat his neck or give him another reward.

As in all things, the 'right' way to catch a pony is right because it works better. If you approach waving the halter, he may decide not to be caught; if you never reward him, he will think you not worth being with; if you do not keep your hand on him, he may decide to leave after grabbing the titbit; if you do not stand as described, you will find it difficult to halter him if he resists. This way, if he does decide to leave, you can stop him by putting your left hand over his nose,

113

Catching: approach confidently, holding a titbit where the pony can see it and the halter or bridle where she cannot. This is an ideal type of first child's pony, stocky, sensible and easy to keep. She is rather overweight, not a bad thing for the time of year (October) though in early spring this type of pony should be thinner to avoid the chance of laminitis when the new grass comes through

pulling his head across your body to the left while pushing back against his chest with your backside. An experienced person can hold even a large and determined horse in this way and halter him at the same time, so practise these movements until they become second nature.

114

Restraining: The pony is keen to escape but Emma uses her weight against his shoulder to slow him down, pulling his nose towards her with her right hand. The pony is wearing overreach boots

Take especial care when catching one pony in a group. Never walk into a group of ponies carrying a bucket, for you may well get knocked down. Try to teach your pony to come to a particular call; if you reward him well he will learn it and reach you before the others do. Getting through a gate when there are other ponies milling around can be difficult, and a small or inexperienced child may need a helper to be safe. Even if it is not strictly your responsibility, make sure the gate works easily.

115

Leading

Do not hold the rope immediately by the head. Ponies like to be able to move their heads to see where they are going, and young or nervous horses get frightened when led or tied up short. Always lead with at least two feet of rope between your hand and the pony's head. Hold the free end of the rope looped across your other hand so it does not trip either of you up. Do not wrap it round your hand or you will get hurt if the pony takes off. If she is likely to do this, tie a big knot in the end of the rope and let it run out, jerking back hard on the knot as she hits the end of the rope.

While leading, walk level with her neck so you can keep an eye on her. Lead from either side, not just from the left. When leading with a bridle, take both reins over her head rather than trying to hold them behind the bit.

When leading a reluctant pony do not stand right in front of him trying to drag him forward. If you face him, he will not understand you plan to step out of the way. Either walk at his shoulder, flicking at his hindquarter with the free end of the rope or a whip held in the left hand, or take a very long lead rope and attach it to the left side of the headcollar. Pass it under his neck and round his rump before running it through the leftside ring of the headcollar. A pull on the rope will then have the effect of pushing him forward if he resists.

A common mistake is to stand in the doorway of a stable or trailer trying to pull the pony forward. From his viewpoint you are right in the way, so naturally he will refuse to budge. Instead, walk right inside making encouraging noises. He may spend some time peering inside into the darkness before coming in, but if you appear safe and happy inside he will be reassured.

A pony does not like to be hustled when she feels unsafe. When startled or frightened, she tries to call your attention to the danger by starting at it. A 'leader' pony would look at the danger, show she was not afraid and walk on. Do the same: do not turn and soothe your pony, nor shout at her, but show clearly that you have indeed seen the 'danger' and consider it safe to pass. When she has passed it, praise her, for you will then encourage her to trust you. When the pony is afraid you must always be confident – or at least appear to be so.

A skittish or nervous pony is more easily led on a longer rather than

116

a shorter rope. In difficult country, for instance, when asking the pony to jump a ditch, use a long rope and stand well clear.

Tying up

Never tie a pony to anything loose or rattly: test it first. Tie to a point preferably level with his head, leaving enough rope for him to be able to look round but not enough for him to be able to put a foot over. If you tie him up too short he is more likely to jerk or panic. If using a halter that slips to fit any size, tie a knot on the left side so it cannot overtighten.

Never tie with anything other than a highwayman's hitch (quick-release knot). If you have one of those geniuses that has learned to release herself quickly, tie the free end of the rope loosely in a half-hitch.

When tying several ponies close together, tie each one to a loop of string that will break if pulled hard, in case fighting breaks out. It is better to have a loose pony than a damaged one.

Releasing

When releasing a pony in the field, take a few steps inside the gate, turn the pony to face the gate, slip off the halter or bridle and feed a titbit. If you simply rip off the halter at the gateway the pony may develop the habit of rushing off, especially when rejoining his friends, kicking out behind him as he goes.

Tacking Up

Bridling

Make sure the pony's head is clean. Take the bridle by the top centre in your left hand and stand by the pony's shoulder, facing forward. Put the reins over her head and take the halter off. Put your right hand between the pony's ears with your arm resting on the top of her neck and pass the bridle into it so that the bridle hangs down the front of her face. If she waves her head about you can control it by clamping her neck between your elbow and your hip, but if you are in the right position she will probably feel thoroughly controlled anyway. You can also hold her nose down with your left hand. When she is still, rest the bit on your left hand and slip your thumb into the upper corner of

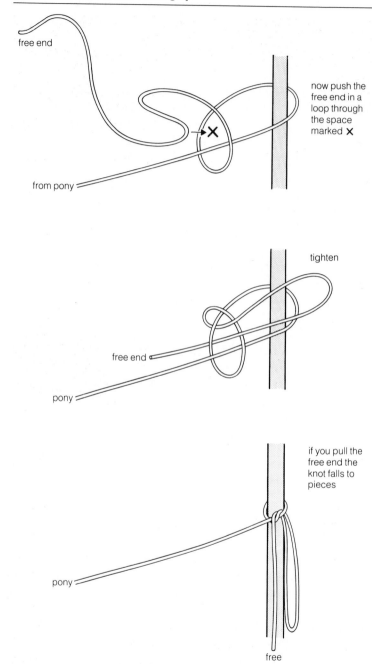

free end

now push the
free end in a
loop through
the space
marked ✗

from pony

tighten

free end

pony

if you pull the
free end the
knot falls to
pieces

pony

free

Figure 22 Highwayman's hitch knot

Putting on a bridle: (1) Sian stands beside the pony with her right hip to his shoulder and her right arm over his neck. With her left thumb she opens his mouth to slip the bit in, cradling it in her fingers. This is a loose-ring snaffle

her mouth. She has no teeth there but she will open her mouth to spit you out. As she does so, slip the bit in, pulling the bridle up with your right hand so the bit does not fall out again. Now pull the headpiece over her ears, taking care of them, fasten the throatlatch, and arrange her forelock so that she is comfortable.

Some people pinch the lower jaw to make the pony open her mouth, but this tends to need more pressure than the thumb-in-the-mouth method. Another way is to hold the bridle by both cheek-pieces, about halfway up, in the right fist, passing the right arm and shoulder under the horse's chin so that the fist can be rested halfway

Putting on a bridle: (2) Too small to reach over the pony's head, Nerys holds both cheekpieces in one hand with her arm round his chin. This is an English hackamore

up the pony's nose from the right. With your left hand put the bit in the pony's mouth, as before. This way allows you to pull the pony's head down with your right hand, so it is useful when bridling a tall pony, but as she does not feel so controlled the pony may be more likely to wave her head about. Also it is more difficult to wriggle from under the pony's neck in order to pull the bridle over her ears.

Whichever method you use, remember that the closer you stand the better, the smoother you work the better, and never to try to put the bit in by pushing it against the pony's teeth. If the pony seems to hate being bitted give her a titbit afterwards.

If the pony is very difficult to bridle, use a headcollar with a buckle on the noseband as well as on the headpiece. You can put a bridle on over one of these and remove it afterwards by undoing both buckles.

Saddling

If the pony is tied up you should always put the saddle on before the bridle. Make sure the pony is clean where the saddle will touch, especially between his front legs. Have the stirrups run up on the leathers and the girth folded over the top of the saddle.

It is easier to put the saddle on from the pony's right side. If you put the saddle on from the left you will have to go round to check the girth is straight before coming back to fasten it. Place the saddle, together with the numnah if you use one, a good hand's breadth up the neck and push it gently backwards until the front is about level with the bottom of the mane. This makes sure that all the hair underneath is facing the right way. If you pull the saddle too far down do not push it back against the hair, but lift it and start again.

Pull the numnah up into the pommel arch so that it is not tight over the withers. This is important: a tight numnah can cause sores just as a badly fitting saddle can. Pull the girth down; make sure it hangs straight, then go round to the other side to do it up. Do not duck under the lead rope if the pony is tied; instead go behind him, keeping very close to his back legs and resting one hand on his rump.

Do up the girth slowly; the strap goes through the top slot of the buckle, not the bottom one. Most ponies take a deep breath while being girthed up, so check the girth is still tight before you get on. Unless you are very strong you will probably not do up a girth too tightly. Run your fingers under it to smooth wrinkled skin.

Unsaddle from the left, first running up the stirrups on the leathers. If the pony has no chance to roll, always rub his back after unsaddling to restore the blood flow.

Unbridling

Take the reins over the pony's head first. Many ponies dash off when the bridle is taken off. Undo the noseband and throatlatch and pull the headpiece gently over the pony's ears. If unbridling in the stable, slide the reins (and martingale neckstrap if used) up to the headpiece before taking the bridle over the pony's ears. Do not rip the bridle off hastily or the pony will throw his head up in the air with his mouth clenched tight (a sign of tension) and so hit himself in the jaw with the bit.

15 Grooming

Ponies do not mind about being clean – in fact, most love rolling in the mud – but they do enjoy the feeling of being groomed. Good grooming stimulates the blood flow in the skin and allows the pores to breathe, making the skin healthier and the coat shinier. It also gives you an opportunity to examine your pony thoroughly.

The Grooming Kit

The absolute minimum grooming kit is a good bristle dandy brush (hard) and a hoofpick. Next add a body brush (soft) and a flat rubber curry comb. A metal or plastic curry comb for cleaning the body brush, a sponge, a mane comb or ordinary hairbrush, a sweat scraper, towel and hoof oil can be added too. Small hands will find a scrubbing brush easier to grasp than a full-size dandy brush.

Minimum Grooming

Pride is the only reason for making your pony spotless before going out for a ride, but you *must* inspect him all over and brush thoroughly any parts the tack will touch. Do not brush wet mud: this causes irritation. Instead, put a little hay covered with a cloth over the wet patch while you do the other bits and it will soon dry.

Put one hand on the pony's neck and start brushing there, using quick, firm strokes. Gentle brushing is useless and will annoy a ticklish pony. At the end of each stroke, flick the brush away from the pony so

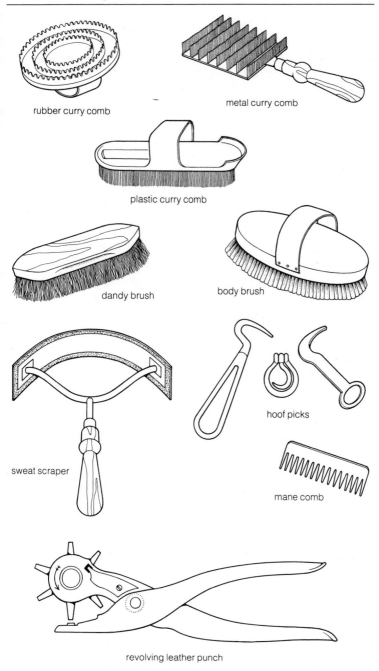

rubber curry comb

metal curry comb

plastic curry comb

dandy brush

body brush

sweat scraper

hoof picks

mane comb

revolving leather punch

Figure 23 Grooming kit

123

that dirt is brushed out, not in. Brush under the saddle area, particularly behind the front legs. Any dirt here easily causes girth galls, and as ponies often sit in the mud they get caked with it. Leave your other hand on the pony's neck or withers as you bend down. Always stay close to him: stabbing at him from two steps away will annoy him.

In summer a body brush can be used; in winter it takes a dandy brush to clean the long winter coat. If you have a rubber curry comb, scrub in circles with it, following with the brush to remove the loosened mud. Go round the back to brush the other side if the pony is tied; leave one hand on his rump and keep close to him so he knows where you are, then he will not kick. Always move slowly but confidently and stay close, so that the pony feels you are with him rather than about to attack him.

When you have brushed both sides, stroke his neck before fondling, then brushing, behind his ears. Some ponies hate having their ears brushed and you may have to use your hand to work out any dried sweat and mud. Rub down his face before brushing with the body brush. Most ponies love to have the underneath of their chins scrubbed hard; most hate to have someone standing at arm's length and reaching nervously towards their heads. Do not use a dandy brush or rubber curry on the face; the skin there is thinner and more sensitive.

Picking up feet

Ponies usually object if you grasp their feet without warning. To pick up a left fore foot: stand facing the pony's rump, close beside him, left hand on his shoulder. Run your hand down his leg, hold the fetlock joint and pick up the foot. If you say 'Foot' every time you do this you will train the pony to pick up his foot at the word. Catch the foot under the toe with your right hand then shift your left underneath it.

When picking out, use the hoofpick from the back to the front of the hoof, cleaning out the grooves on each side of the frog. If the pony picks up his foot before you get to his fetlock, catch it under the toe immediately. Do not be surprised, for he is only trying to help. If he refuses to pick his foot up, push your hip against his shoulder, throwing his weight on to the opposite side at the same time as trying again. Some ponies respond if you pinch the back tendon above the fetlock.

To pick up a back foot, stand close to his hindquarter facing the rear

Picking up a back foot. If you stand in the right place, facing backwards with your feet level with the middle of his belly, the pony cannot hurt you even if he kicks. This pony, which is trained to be ground-tied (never leave your reins hanging like that on a pony that is not!) is rather annoyed. Notice the good hayrack on the wall beyond

and run your hand down his leg, exactly as for a front foot. Many novices are nervous about picking up back feet but this only makes a pony nervous too. If you are nervous or if you know the pony will kick out, stand a little farther forward, level with the front of the hindquarter, and pull the leg forward as you pick it up. Hold it forward for a moment until you can feel it relax before pulling it back and picking it out.

If you are standing in the right place the pony cannot possibly hurt

125

you even if he does kick out, so there is no need to be nervous. Do not let him scare you off by waving a foot at you: simply stand yourself in the right place and try again. Even if you fail several times, keep trying, and you will find the pony will suddenly give up; next time he will give up even sooner. Do not shout at him or hit him, but praise him when he does the right thing (not before).

You do not need to pick out his feet every time you ride, but you do need to see that there is nothing stuck in the bottom of them.

If you want to oil his hooves use proper hoof oil, not sump oil, which does them no good.

In snow, clean the feet thoroughly, dry the soles carefully and paint them with thick grease or smear them with lard. This stops the snow forming a ball inside the shoe.

Thorough Grooming

Start at the neck or shoulder, for this is where ponies groom their friends. Brush firmly and briskly, making sure you cover the whole body. Keep your free hand on the pony, for this reassures her. As you work backwards, stay close and face the rear. Some ponies are ticklish under the belly; do not brush too lightly as it tickles even more, and do not leap back if she objects. The inside of the back legs often gets sweaty and dirty. Remove this grime with a body brush, starting at the top and holding the tail as you work.

A rubber curry comb is used to scrub in circles before mud is brushed off. Plastic ones are used only where the coat is thick. Metal curry combs are for cleaning body brushes, not horses: after every dozen or so brushstrokes, scrape the brush over the curry comb several times, then turn the comb sideways and knock out the dirt with the edge of your brush.

The mane and forelock can be brushed with a dandy brush, or combed if thin. A mane comb will only tear at a thick mane: use a good hairbrush instead. Tease out tangles with your fingers; if they are bad and keep reknotting, use a little silicone wax spray on them before untangling them, but do warn the pony by showing him the can and demonstrating first, or he may be alarmed by the snake hissing on his neck.

Use a dandy brush on the tail. Stand to one side of the pony's rump, pull the tail towards you and release a few strands at a time to be brushed. You may find combing with your fingers more effective.

You should groom your pony thoroughly every week even when you are not riding her, for it means that you examine every inch of her and will feel any lumps or cuts that appear. Notice any changes in the way her skin feels: the skin shows when she is sickening for something before any other symptoms appear.

Sponging
Sponging the nostrils and ears is again more necessary with a stabled pony. Do not do it while she is tied or she may jerk back and then fight the rope. Sponge the dock area too. Geldings benefit from having the sheath sponged inside but most are shy about this: it is only necessary if the sheath becomes smelly or if you can see that he is filthy there when he passes water. If he has difficulty in passing water it may be that the passage is clogged with a 'bean' of old grease.

A thin-skinned pony that has sweated a lot in summer will appreciate being sponged with lots of water between and inside the back legs. The hairless skin is very thin there and can become scalded and uncomfortable.

Wisping

A wisp is used to dry a pony that is wet from rain or sweat. Take a large handful of straw and pull it out, twisting it with both hands as you do so, until a loose rope begins to form. When this is a foot or two long, put one end under your foot and continue to twist the other until the rope tightens. Turn it into a figure 8 and tuck the ends in. You will now have a matted pad of straw. It is easier to make a wisp out of hay, but not as good for drying. Rub and scrub at your pony to dry her off.

You can also wisp a dry pony: she will enjoy it, especially if she is stabled as she gets no chance to roll and rub.

Clipping

If your pony has a heavy winter coat and is in hard use so he sweats up a lot, you may need to clip him to avoid his getting a chill in winter.

127

Making a wisp. Form the straw or hay into a loose rope and twist it round, putting one end under your foot as it tightens. Then tie the rope into a knot

The simplest, minimum clip is a strip taken down the underside of the neck and belly. A trace-high clip removes more hair, to halfway up the body, while a hunter clip (for a stabled horse only) removes hair from everywhere except the legs and under the saddle. A trace-clipped pony must wear a New Zealand rug while outside in winter.

Do not try clipping unless you have watched and been advised by an expert. Many ponies hate being clipped so do not try on your own without help. Do not clip unless really necessary, and never clip the whiskers and ears, whatever you are advised. The whiskers are an important sense organ.

Hunter clip on a good quality Thoroughbred horse: superb shoulder, withers and hindquarters but the typical light bone of the Thoroughbred

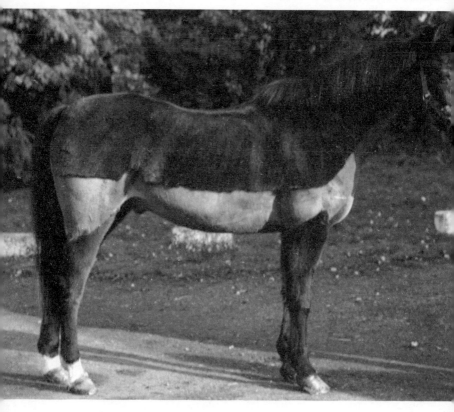

Trace clip on a cob-type pony

Strapping

Strapping is vigorous grooming usually done with the hands, although a mitt or cloth is sometimes used. Thorough strapping removes the oily scurf that waterproofs a pony's coat, so it is necessary only when the pony is stabled. It increases blood flow through the skin and tones up the muscles underneath, so the effect is as refreshing and beneficial as a good massage. A sick, stabled pony is greatly helped by a good strapping every day. Daily strapping for three weeks raises a tremendous sheen on the coat, a deeper-than-skin-deep gloss. However, if the pony is kept outdoors the grease should not be totally removed from his coat.

First, loosen dirt, scurf and hair with the rubber curry comb and brush off until you think the pony is clean. Cup your hands slightly (for authenticity spit on them and rub them together) and, starting at the shoulder, half-stroke, half-slap the pony with each hand in turn, as hard as she will let you and with a good rhythm. At first she will probably be rather taken aback, but most horses come to love being strapped and brace themselves delightedly against the slaps. You will find that the scurf collects as grey grime on your hands. Rub it off and carry on, working thoroughly over every body area except the belly. Brush, strap and brush again twice more if the pony is stabled. After a few days you will find she will come as clean as a newly washed pony after the third strapping, and will glow with well-being.

Shampooing

Shampooing is the lazy way to have a clean pony; and like most lazy ways it is not as good as the best way: strapping. Washing removes all the grease in a pony's coat, so you should not wash an outdoor pony more than two or three times a summer and never if it is liable to rain in the next few days. Only wash if the weather is warm. Use tepid water, rinse off well with a hosepipe, and dry with a sweat scraper (a car windscreen-wiper blade makes a good substitute). Take care not to get water down his ears. A little silicone wax spray worked into the damp coat improves the sheen, makes it last longer, and waterproofs the pony until he replaces his natural grease.

When shampooing the mane, rinse it out thoroughly; conditioner helps. Wash the tail in a bucket of tepid water and rinse well.

Ground-tying

A good practice when grooming is to leave the pony untied and stand on the lead rope with one foot. If the pony tries to move, jerk the lead rope downwards and tell her 'stand'. If you persist with this you will train your pony to ground-tie, that is, believe she is tied to the ground when the lead rope is dropped. It is not a good idea to tie the pony to the ground or she may panic and get her legs rope-burned, but standing on the rope makes her think she is tied (see also page 163).

131

16 Basic Riding

Riding a pony is not like driving a car; a pony is not a machine that you operate and keep in working trim with a little maintenance. He is a living being, as full of hopes, fears, doubts and fun as yourself, only with rather less intellectual ability. A pony and rider are a partnership. On your side you give him food, safety, freedom from worms and illness; he gives you his strength and energy. You give him guidance; he will tell you what his excellent eyes, ears and nose tell him, if you care to listen. But he will work against you if you do not give him your understanding and appreciation. Always remember that, like yourself, he will work better for praise than punishment; he will overcome his fears better if he is understood rather than bullied; he will respond better if you ask rather than force him; in short, he would rather be your friend than your slave.

Mounting

Always wear a proper hat, and fasten the chin strap. When about to ride a strange pony, spend a few moments messing about near him, talking to him, checking his tack, scratching his neck, so that he has time to smell and hear you. Make sure the girth is tight; pull the stirrups down on the leathers. Put your fingertips on the bar which holds the stirrup leather and, with your arm straight, measure the stirrup against the underside of your arm. If the stirrup fits neatly into your armpit the length is about right.

Standing on the pony's left, take the reins in your left hand, making sure they are short enough to stop the pony wandering off, and grasp a chunk of mane in front of the saddle. Face the pony's rump, put your left foot in the stirrup, your right hand on the far side of the seat of the saddle, and spring up. Do not try to pull yourself up or you will unbalance the pony; instead, hop a couple of times and bounce up. Try not to kick the pony's bottom or crash down on his back as you land in the saddle.

By facing the pony's rear you can still mount easily even if he moves off, as his movement will help you swing up. If you know he will move off, keep your left rein shorter than the right, for then he will move round you. If you have a joker that insists on biting your bottom, face his head, put both your hands on the pommel of the saddle, and spring into the saddle that way. It is more difficult to stop a pony from moving off that way. However, never try to mount facing the pony's side or you will stick your toe in his side and he will obediently walk off with you hopping sideways.

It is normal to mount from the left side, a habit persisting from the days when gentlemen wore swords (if you try mounting from the right with a sword on your left hip you will soon see why); American Indians, who carried bows in their left hands, normally jumped on from the right. However, it is useful, and sometimes necessary, to be able to mount from the right, too, and to have a pony that finds this acceptable, so do not worry too much about which side you mount from.

When jumping on bareback, keep the reins short, grasp the mane in your left hand and if possible hook your left elbow across the pony's neck; rest your right hand on his back and jump on to your stomach before trying to put your right leg across his back. Your elbows play a helpful role in getting you on. You can take the mane in the left hand, take a step back and vault straight on, but you will only succeed if you are very athletic.

The Seat

A 'good' position or seat is one which allows the pony to move at any pace over any ground without your weight interfering with him. This means you must always be in balance. There are different seats for different types of riding: for jumping, racing, polo, dressage and Western. You may sometimes find that the advice you are given is confusing, for different teachers all regard their own method as the only correct one. In all horsemanship it is more helpful to try to understand why things work as they do rather than merely taking someone else's word for what is 'correct'. An Olympic dressage rider would find his correctness all out of place in the Grand National. What is right, surely, is what works best most often.

The seat and aids given here are the most universal possible: you will find they work with horses anywhere and that you can easily adapt to suit special variations from this central position.

Sitting on the pony with your feet out of the stirrups, wriggle about freely, rocking from side to side and stretching your legs down and your head up. In this way you will naturally settle yourself deep into the saddle and find the best position. Now turn your toes up, without clutching the pony with your legs. Look down and see where the stirrups are. They should be an inch or so above your feet, no more. Rest the ball of your foot on the stirrup; do not push your foot right in. If your stirrups are too short you will tend to stand on them too much, pushing yourself up off the pony's back; if they are too long they are useless.

Sit tall. Imagine you are pushing the top of your head up to the sky, so the middle of you is long and free. It is this freedom in your waist area that means the lower half of you can move with the pony without affecting the top half. Most beginners are far too tight in the lower back. You should be able to roll your hips forward and back without moving your shoulders.

Press your heels down, relaxing your ankle so that your weight drops into your heel. This changes the shape of the muscles higher in the leg so you fit better round the pony. You can feel the difference if you stand on a step, with only the front half of your foot on the tread. At first you will try to stand on your toes, but if you relax your ankle you will find that you are standing on your heel although it is unsupported. With your knees slightly bent, you will keep your balance perfectly. Your calf muscles will feel stretched, your upper leg relaxed. On the pony again, with your feet in the stirrups, stand first on your toes, then on your heels. You will find that with your heels down your knee stays against the saddle better, and that as you stand up in the stirrups it keeps you firm. Your toes should point forwards. If they turn out you will tend to grip with your calf, a dreadful mistake as the pony will go faster and faster.

134

Good all-purpose seat, with long leg, straight back, and hands
well-positioned. Ideally the lower leg should be further back, bringing
shoulder, hip and heel into a straight line

Later you will find that this heels-down position is very important when going down steep hills or stopping a runaway horse, for in both cases you need to lean back and brace your foot against the stirrup. If your toes are down your foot will slip through the stirrup, a very dangerous position.

Your shoulder and hip should be in line above your heel, for it is only in this position that you can stand up in the stirrups without being unbalanced. Stand up and down several times, fast, to check that this is so. If your lower leg is too far forward you will find that you cannot do this without leaning forward or pulling on the reins, either of which upsets the pony.

Wriggle and roll your shoulders to relax your shoulder and arms, then pick up the reins. They should be held as shown on page 135. Your hands should stay low, so that there is a straight line from the bit to your elbow. Your hands and arms should stay relaxed, for any tension will be uncomfortable for the pony. Moreover, if your shoulders and arms tense your hands will tend to come up so that the pull on the bit will come from a different angle and no longer be effective.

The reins should be long enough so that as the pony walks along there is no pull on them, but if you tighten your hand and pull back a little you will put pressure on the bit. Do not worry about 'contact' at this stage (see chapter 18). Your aim should be to use the reins as little as possible, concentrating instead on your seat, so that you feel safe at all paces whether you are holding the reins or not. You cannot develop good, sensitive hands without this independent seat. Beginners tend to want to clutch the reins tightly, relying on them for balance. Your balance should come from a good seat and supple back, not your hands.

If you are a real beginner you will do much better if someone leads you along, preferably over rough ground, for your first few hours in the saddle, for then you can concentrate on keeping your heels down and learning to relax and move with the pony before trying to control him as well.

The Aids

These are the ways in which we give directions to the horse. The natural aids are the seat and weight, the voice, the legs, and the hands; the artificial aids are the whip and spurs.

To understand clearly how to use the natural aids, remember first how a pony moves: his engine is his hindquarters and he turns by pushing his front end round. Second, he always moves so as to make himself more comfortable. If you put pressure on any part of him, he will move away from that pressure.

Your seat and weight affect the pony's balance and speed. Leaning back puts more weight on his hindquarters and slows him down; leaning forward when your legs push as well frees his hindquarters for more effort and makes him go faster. Leaning forward without using your legs can tip his balance forward and downward so he seems heavy. Leaning to the side overbalances him so he moves to that side to put himself under you again. Pushing forward with the seat drives him forward.

The legs control what is behind you: the hindquarters. Squeezing with both legs makes a pony go faster. If you squeeze with each leg in turn the pony will lengthen his stride. If you squeeze without letting go he will change pace, from a walk to a trot or a trot to a canter. Pushing with one leg just behind the girth makes the pony move over: if you push with the right leg he will shift over to the left, without changing his general direction. For instance, if you want him to walk on a grass verge on the left of a road, squeeze with your right leg. You should not need to kick a pony: a good squeeze works better than a thumping kick. However, some ponies are far more sensitive to the leg than others.

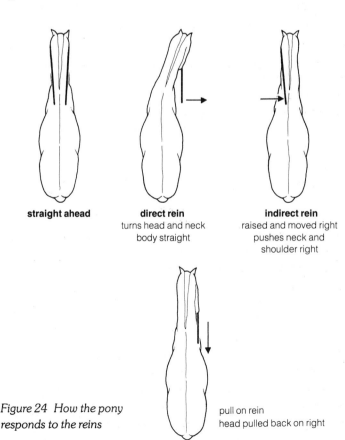

straight ahead

direct rein
turns head and neck
body straight

indirect rein
raised and moved right
pushes neck and
shoulder right

Figure 24 How the pony responds to the reins

pull on rein
head pulled back on right

137

The hands, via the reins, control what is in front of you: the head, neck and shoulder. By closing and stiffening your hand as you move it outwards (direct rein) you put pressure on the bit, and the pony will therefore bend his head towards the pull. By moving your hand inwards towards his neck (indirect rein) you press the rein against his neck and shoulder, and he will then turn them away from the push.

Most beginners use the reins far too harshly and depend on them too much, which tends to make the pony resist rather than give. The more you use your legs the less you have to use your reins, and the pleasanter the effect.

Clicking encourages a pony to move on. In some circles it is considered rude to click your pony on in public in case others move on too. Most ponies also know what 'Whoa' means, but they will not take any notice if you scream it. 'Whoa' should always be a slow, calm command. All ponies take notice of the tone of your voice, and really well-trained ones will change pace entirely by voice command. It is extremely useful to teach your pony what you mean by 'walk on', 'whoa', 'stand', 'good', 'behave yourself' and 'you're tied up', because you then have some control even from a distance. Use your voice to praise your pony when he has done well.

The whip is used to show a pony that he must respond to the leg. It is not for beating him with when you think he has been naughty. Hold a whip as shown in the photograph on page 13. With an unwilling pony, use your legs first, then, if he does not respond, tap his shoulder (or behind your heel if the whip is long enough). Many beginners jerk the rein as they use the whip, and the pony ends up doubly hurt and confused, so do not use a whip unless you are sure that it is not your bad riding that is the trouble. However, many old, wise ponies behave better if you simply carry a whip without using it.

Spurs are not for novices.

Applying the Aids

To stop

With your heels well down, lean back and tighten both reins. At first you may lean too far back rather inelegantly, but later you will find that all you really have to do is use your back to push down with your seat. The commonest beginner's mistake is to use only the reins. This does not work. The beginner, feeling nervous, usually leans forward and tightens his legs, which drives the pony on faster so he 'runs away'. Make sure that if your leg moves at all it goes forward, away from the pony's side, rather than back into it.

You cannot stop a determined pony without leaning back and using your weight. In the field, try seeing if you can stop your pony by weight alone.

To turn

A pony can turn in several different ways, which is at first confusing, but if you remember what your aids are doing you will not make mistakes.

To circle to the left while moving: you will want the pony's hindquarters to go left, his shoulders and neck to go left, and his head to lead the way. As his movement starts from the back, press just behind the girth with your right leg. Use your left rein directly and your right rein against the shoulder, by moving both hands slightly to the left, as if you were turning yourself. Do not cross your right hand over the neck or you will pull the bit on that side and confuse the pony. A common mistake is to pull on the direct (in this case left) rein only. This asks the pony to move his head but not his body, so a well-trained pony will continue straight on with his head turned. The use of the opposite (indirect or neck) rein is frowned on in some circles of English riding, but it works much better than using the direct rein alone and is also more universal. If you practise riding with your reins in one hand you will find that you are automatically using the indirect rein. In polo and Western riding, as well as in most fast riding, the neck rein is used more than the direct rein. Learn to use both.

To turn round at a standstill: here you want the pony to swivel so he is facing in the opposite direction. For instance, you want his neck and shoulders to go left but his hindquarters to go right. Use your left leg behind the girth to start the movement and follow it by moving both reins to the left.

A common mistake is to use the same aids as for a moving turn, which in this case would simply ask the pony to curl himself into a knot.

If you use only the left leg while asking him not to move with your hands, you will ask him to do a turn on the forehand, where he leaves

139

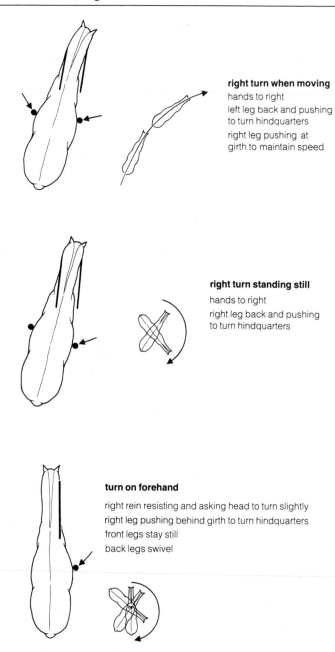

right turn when moving

hands to right
left leg back and pushing
to turn hindquarters
right leg pushing at
girth to maintain speed

right turn standing still

hands to right
right leg back and pushing
to turn hindquarters

turn on forehand

right rein resisting and asking head to turn slightly
right leg pushing behind girth to turn hindquarters
front legs stay still
back legs swivel

Figure 25 Use of aids while turning

his front legs in the same place but walks his hind legs in a half circle round them.

When turning, then, always use your legs before your hands. Do not lean forward anxiously or you will tip the pony's weight forward and make him more difficult to turn (see chapter 4).

Problems

At first you may find that the pony does not respond well. This is more likely to be due to your stiffness, anxiety and lack of coordination than to disobedience on her part. Do not think that you have to pull harder on the reins: almost certainly you need to push harder with your legs. Practise turns and stops in a quiet place, experimenting to find out the balance between leg, hand and weight aids that the pony understands best. When she responds well, stop and praise her. Always use the gentlest aids possible, especially with your hands, increasing the pressure only if the pony does not respond. If you always start with the lightest touch you will find that the pony comes to respond to that; if you give thumping kicks and yank at the reins you will make her sullen and disobedient.

The walk

Use your legs to encourage the pony to walk out freely and briskly. Let your hands move with her head as she walks along or you will jab her in the mouth at every stride.

The trot

There are two ways of trotting, the rising or post trot and the sitting trot. The rising trot is most easily done at a good pace, when it gets bouncy. You stand in the stirrups for every other step; the bounce helps you to rise. First practise standing and sitting in the stirrups at a standstill, then at a walk. Feel the rhythm of the pony's front feet, or watch one shoulder coming back towards you, counting the paces, 'one, two, one, two', then changing that to 'up, down, up, down'. Now urge the pony into a trot without losing the rhythm, which will naturally speed up. When you have got the timing right it feels smooth.

It is a great help to have someone lead you when you first try. To avoid jerking on the reins, steady your hands by grasping the mane several inches up the neck. Do not hold the front of the saddle, for if you do your reins will be too long for you to stop. It is a good idea to put a strap round the pony's neck and hook your little fingers through it for support if you have a bouncy trotter.

Common beginner's mistakes: pulling the reins to help you stand in the stirrups, when of course the pony will get fed up; leaning forward too much; letting your legs swing about when you stand up. The knee and lower leg need to be firm for a rising trot.

The sitting trot is easiest when the pony is trotting slowly. Simply relax and sit down. At first you will probably find this difficult because you will be too stiff in your back and legs. Relax. Being anxious makes you bounce more, and the more you hold on with your legs the worse it gets. You will find it easier to lean back at first, and to straighten up as you get better. It is free movement in your lower back that stops you bouncing.

When you have mastered a sitting trot, practise it without stirrups, for this helps you to develop good balance and seat.

The canter
From a trot, sit down and push with your seat as you use your legs. At first it is easier to stand in the stirrups, holding the mane, until you get the feel of the rhythm. However, you should be able to sit firmly in the saddle without bouncing. One way of doing this is to imagine you have the winning Premium Bond under your seat: make sure it stays there. Some people find it easier to rock forward and back, as if on a rocking horse, but this looks ugly and makes the pony canter heavily. It should only be your hips that rock. Again, you will find that this depends on being loose in the small of your back. You cannot sit to a canter if you are tight in the thigh.

It is much easier to canter uphill than on the flat at first.

The gallop
The gallop often follows the canter without any obvious change. As the canter gets faster, stand slightly in the stirrups and lean forward. When you are going to slow down, sit down firmly and lean back, with your heels well down, or you will overbalance forward.

Backing
Backing is not particularly easy for ponies and as many have been forced back, rather than being asked properly, they become more

difficult. Ask the pony not to move forward with your hands, by keeping the rein firm, and then ask him to move with your legs. Logically he must go backwards. Saying 'back' at the same time usually helps. It is no use trying to pull him back.

If the pony backs without your asking, release the reins and push him forward with your legs. Pulling the reins will only make him back faster.

Steep uphill

Stand in the stirrups, lean well forward with your hands halfway up the pony's neck, take a firm grasp of a chunk of mane and give the pony his head. If you pull on the reins the pony will start slithering backwards. Banks are great fun and good for both of you.

Steep downhill

Coming off a bank, lean forward with your feet forward. Down a long steep hill, lean back, push your lower leg forward with your heel well down, and give the pony her head. She cannot see where to put her feet unless you let her put her head low; having your weight back will steady her, and having your feet forward means you can keep your position better.

Mistakes

Common beginner's mistakes in riding: too much rein used, too harshly, letting your hands fly up when nervous and leaning forward. Unfortunately it is a natural human reaction to lean forward when you are nervous, but this is exactly the wrong thing to do on a pony as it makes her go faster. Whenever you feel nervous, always lean back, keeping your lower leg well out of the pony's side, for then things will calm down.

17 Hacking

Always check your girth before moving off, as many ponies take a deep breath when first girthed up. (Check again ten minutes later.) Check, too, that you have not crossed the reins when putting them over the pony's head, or you will rapidly embarrass yourself.

Many ponies are wilful when ridden in their home field, so if you want to practise without going out for a ride it is better to go into another field or you may find yourself having difficulty leaving the gate, or charging madly back to it. Most ponies greatly enjoy going out and like exploring new places. If you have a new pony and are not sure how he will react when out, take him for a walk instead. This will help you get to know each other and to build up a bond between you. There is no harm, either, in dismounting and leading your pony if you are nervous of what lies ahead: after all, a pony has no idea what you intend to do next. Don't, however, get into the habit of leaping off whenever the pony plays up a little or he will learn to take advantage of that.

For a novice, exercises before going out settle you into the saddle. Stand up and sit down several times, making sure your legs and heels stay in the right place. Lie forward along the pony's neck; touch his ears; clasp your hands round his neck, again making sure your lower leg does not move. Touch your toes, first with the hand on the same side, then with the opposite hand, keeping a check on that lower leg. With both reins in one hand, swing the other arm vigorously and shake your hand and wrist to make them free and relaxed. Lie backwards with your head on the pony's rump. Stretch your legs down; circle your ankles; rock your hips freely.

Most of these exercises are best done in the field facing the gate for

Exercises before going out. Joanna, hands raised, stretches her body up and legs down, rolling her hips from side to side to find the right place in the saddle; Emily stretches and arches her back by lying back

the pony is then unlikely to move, but you may need someone to hold him.

You should also be able to do these exercises at a walk and, finally, at a gallop with your reins in one hand, without pulling them.

Practise opening and closing the gate without getting off, thinking carefully about the aids you use to position the pony. Never try to shut a gate by reaching back over the pony's rump for it, for unless you

145

have arms like a gorilla or are riding a ludicrously small pony the gate is bound to hit his hocks.

When you are out, remember that riders have an unfortunate reputation for being haughty and rude. Many people are frightened of large animals, so slow down and give pedestrians a wide berth so they do not feel you are about to run them down. Do not ride across fields without permission, and even then ride with respect; even the most generous of farmers get annoyed by trails of muddy hoof prints across their fields, at stock disturbed and crops damaged. Leave gates exactly as you find them, ride round the edges of fields, and report any animals in distress straightaway, and you may even find your riding opportunities increase.

Bridleways, along which riders have a right of way, are supposed to be marked on Ordnance Survey maps. Often, though, even OS maps are incorrect and the only way to be certain you are on a bridleway is by checking with the Highways Department of your local county (or metropolitan borough) council. It is also to them that you should report if you find a bridleway blocked, fenced or otherwise impassable. You may also ride along tracks marked as RUPPs (road used as a public path) and BOATs (byeway open to all traffic).

Having the right to ride along a bridleway does not entitle you to abuse it. If you gallop along a track in wet weather you will ruin it, for yourself and others. Keeping bridleways open and in good repair is important to all riders. In many areas there are bridleways groups who give information about local bridleways and work to maintain them. It is in your interest to join one.

Try to vary your ride, thinking of unexpected changes so your pony does not become set in his ways. Variety keeps a pony interested and awake. Practise going up and down the steepest hills you can find, for this improves your seat; find logs to step over, difficulties to pick your way through.

You should never end up accepting a pony's refusal to do something. This means that, first, you must always think twice before urging your pony on, asking yourself: is it possible? Is it safe? Secondly, once you have decided to go on, you must not give up.

Suppose, say, you decide to cross a stream. Approach it confidently, knowing that you are going to go across. Be ready to slip the reins so the pony may sniff and peer if she seems doubtful, but be quick to gather them up again so you do not lose control. While she is

146

Wild Welsh mountain pony mare crossing a dip puts her head down to see where she is going. When riding across rough country let your reins slip through your fingers whenever your pony wants to inspect the ground, or she cannot see properly and will refuse to cross ditches or difficult places

investigating, praise her and stop pushing her on; the moment she decides to move, make sure she goes forward. Do not let her turn her head away from the stream; keep pushing her forward, except at those moments when she is sniffing. The moment she makes the slightest move forward, praise her and keep pushing. Many ponies refuse only when they feel that you too are doubtful about the idea; many will refuse with greater and greater determination. However, if you meet each refusal with equal determination, you will find that the pony suddenly gives up and goes forward. If you find you really cannot get her to go forward, dismount, take the reins over her head and lead her forwards. Usually she will see that it is safe for you and follow meekly. It is a good idea to come back and repeat the crossing mounted, just to prove your point.

If you make a habit of praising your pony whenever she has done something difficult or that frightened her, you will find she becomes more willing and adventurous. If you only scold her when she has done something you do not like, and go on demanding without

147

Crossing a deep ditch, the pony wants to stretch and lower his head to examine the difficulties. Joanna keeps pushing him forwards but leaves his head well alone although her reins are just short enough for her to regain control if he decides to back out. When he takes the plunge she will grasp the mane in front of her hands so she does not slip back and pull the reins as he leaps up the steep bank the other side. She trusts him not to refuse or drop her, for he trusts her not to hurt or unbalance him

rewarding her, you will find she becomes sullen and uncooperative.

If your pony becomes excited or nervous, try not to be alarmed. It is important that you remain calm: any nervousness on your part will upset her more. It is unfortunate that the natural reaction, leaning forward, clutching the reins and clinging tightly with the legs, is exactly the wrong one. Lean back; keep your heels pressed down and your hands calm; relax your legs; keep facing the difficulty and try to reassure the pony. Your weight will help prevent her from trying to dash past whatever scares her.

Many cold-blooded ponies show their nervousness by stopping rather than by dancing about. Ponies cannot see well while they are moving, so in strange places many stop to have a good look before going on. Do not instantly lose your temper or try to force him on before he is ready; rather, put your hand on his neck and talk to him, until you feel his tension die down. Then he will be ready to go on if you ask.

Most ponies greatly prefer to go out in company. They are usually calmer, bolder and more joyful, though some mares can be silly in company when they are in season. If you plan to ride with someone else and are not sure how the ponies will take to each other, leave them tied a little distance apart, preferably with some food each, so they can watch and smell each other. If they want to meet more closely, stand well aside as you lead them to each other at an angle. Ponies, especially mares, sometimes strike out with a forefoot, squealing, when they meet. This is not an expression of hatred but of excitement, and they will almost certainly ride out happily together; but if you or another pony's leg gets in the way of a rapidly moving forefoot, it hurts. Watch out for kicking too.

When riding with others, remember to wait for the person closing a gate behind you, for if you go on his pony will get overexcited.

If you meet strangers riding when you are out, keep your distance. You have no idea whether their ponies are friendly or well controlled, while even the best-behaved stallion becomes difficult if you wander right up to him.

If you want to tie your pony while out on a ride take a halter with you. Never tie a pony up by his bridle, for if he pulls back he will hurt himself badly and break his reins. You can let him go with his bridle on if you take the reins over his head, pull them through the bridle below his ear, and make a knot of the slack so he cannot step on it.

149

You should never let him go with the reins loose or trailing, nor should you leave the saddle on, lest he roll on it and break the tree.

On your way home, always slow down for the last half mile. This will cool the pony off and discourage him from galloping madly homewards. If he is really hot, dismount, slacken the girth, and lead him the last half mile or so to cool him. You cannot put a hot, wet pony in a field at nightfall or he may catch a chill. This is a particular problem in winter when his shaggy coat makes him sweat; and, once wet, it takes a long time to dry. In this case, dry him by rubbing vigorously with a wisp.

If you are keeping your pony in, it is nevertheless a good idea to turn him out for half an hour or so if possible, to cool and roll. If he has come back hot he will sweat up in the stable; he may even break out after you think you have dried him thoroughly, so check him an hour or so later to make sure he has stayed dry.

When planning a ride, remember: you will strain a pony's legs if you gallop him when he is unfit, or even if you trot hard for a long way on the road. Most ponies love a gallop but get overexcited if you overdo it. A hot pony must not drink gallons of cold water and then be asked to move fast. A pony will not go for more than a couple of hours before wanting a snack, unless he is fit and having hard food. A good long steady trot at the beginning of a ride settles an excitable pony better than trying to hold him to a walk. Always lean forwards, not backwards, under low branches.

18 Improving Your Seat and Hands

It is impossible to be a good rider unless you have light, sensitive hands, and equally it is impossible to have good hands unless you have a firm, independent seat. By 'independent' we mean that your seat is not dependent on your hands, that you do not need your hands for balance or staying on.

The clearest test of an independent seat is of course to ride without reins. This can be done on a lunge rein but you will need another person to help you.

First, try lungeing your pony without a rider. You will need a lunge line or light rope at least 20 feet long. Attach it to the back of the headcollar if you have no cavesson, and ask the pony to walk, trot and canter in circles round you. Start by standing the pony still and backing away from him, level with his girth, for 10–15 feet. Ask him to go in a circle anticlockwise (most ponies find it easier to move in this direction) by holding the rein in your left hand, saying 'Walk on' sharply, and clicking the fingers of your right hand towards his hindquarters. If he has been lunged before he will know what to do; if not you may need a lunge whip or long whippy stick to encourage him to move and to keep him from wandering in to you. You will also find it helpful to have a friend leading him on the opposite side. Bring the whip level with his hocks to shoo him forward; wriggle it on the ground if necessary, but *do not* hit him with it. If he starts to come in, point the whip at his shoulder.

When you say 'Whoa', drop the whip, stand absolutely still yourself and reward him when he stops. The first few times, choose moments when he seems about to stop anyway, then you will be able to praise his 'obedience'. Ideally, he should learn to change pace at your word,

151

but for lungeing with a rider all he must do is move reliably in circles round the lunger.

Now ask your helper to lunge the pony while you ride. Tie the reins in a knot and let go of them. You should be able to swing your arms in circles, hold them up or out, swing your whole body with your arms out, stand in your stirrups without losing your balance, and touch your toes, all at a walk, trot and canter. You will find this hard at first. As your balance improves, repeat the exercises without stirrups. Ride round with your arms folded. If you find this unnerving, you will realize how much you depend on your reins. After all, the pony cannot run away and you do not need to turn him, so why the worry?

Riding without stirrups or bareback also improves your balance. However, when riding bareback make sure you are not clinging on with your calves. Ride by balance rather than grip, feeling the pony's movement and rhythm and allowing yourself to move freely with it. You cannot trot bareback if you grip with your legs: instead you have to balance on the base of your spine. It is easier if you lean back at first.

If you are lucky and live among mountains or hills, use the slopes. Riding up and down steep slopes and picking your way through difficult places gives you a better seat faster than years of riding on relatively flat ground. It makes you loosen up so that you are more supple while sitting firmly; you will also realise that you cannot cling to the reins or the pony will not go, for he needs his head free in tricky places. Pick out steep places to go up and down; turn off the track and find challenges, and your body will learn without your having to think too much about it. This will also benefit your pony, suppling and strengthening him so he uses his body well too.

Once you feel confident about riding without reins or on a loose rein, concentrate on improving your hands. Novices are almost always heavy-handed, using too much pressure on the rein. This comes partly from a natural human feeling that hands are what you control things with; partly from tension, for a beginner is usually tense and tension does not allow you to be sensitive; and partly from not using your legs and weight enough, so that more pressure on the rein does have to be used. By riding without reins or a loose rein, you can realize that your hands are not so necessary: by thinking about your shoulder, elbow and wrist, you can learn to relax them so that you give to the least pull on the rein. By remembering to use your legs

Exercises on the lunge improve seat and balance. This pony lunges well and does not need a whip: Niki stands in the centre, holding the lunge line loosely coiled in her left hand while swinging the free end of the line gently behind the pony to remind her to keep trotting. Joanna does her exercises bareback. They should have tied the reins in a knot, lest the pony step in them

before your hands, and even by trying to turn the pony by leg and balance only, you will again lighten your hands.

Always use your rein smoothly and gently, applying the least possible pressure and only increasing it if the pony does not respond. Some ponies have hard or insensitive mouths after years of being ridden badly, but it is surprising how far even an old pony's mouth will recover its feeling if treated gently.

The idea of contact is greatly misunderstood. It means having a feel, a way of communicating, with the pony's mouth through the rein. Unfortunately most beginners tend to clutch the reins too hard so that their idea of a 'feel' is more like a kilo weight on the rein. A pony can feel your hand move through the weight of the rein alone,

153

as long as the rein is not dangling loose. Yet most novice riders cannot feel when the pony's head moves, as it does, for instance, at every step she takes when walking. It is not unusual to see a novice riding along with one rein shorter than the other so that the pony's head is turned to one side. In other words, the pony is more sensitive than the rider: she can feel when the rider cannot. Until you have as much feeling as the pony, until you find that your hand is so relaxed that it is moving, yielding, at each step the pony takes, you do not have enough sensitivity to try to take a contact.

However, as you develop this sensitivity you will find that you are shortening your reins, since this gives you more constant control and a more constant flow of feeling between you and the pony. You should feel as if you have a minnow on the end of a fishing line; you should treat the pony's mouth as if it were full of eggs, which can take a fair amount of pressure as long as it is not applied sharply. In more advanced riding, such as dressage and eventing, a stronger contact is often needed because the horse is taught to move in a slightly different manner; besides, these strong, energetic, well-fed performance horses take a fair amount of holding or they simply charge away. For ordinary cross-country riding you need only the minimum of contact with your hands. What is more usually lacking in the rider is active legs which keep the pony moving briskly. He should not slop along as too many do, and he certainly does not need a dead weight on the rein, that is so often thought to be 'contact'.

In most parts of the world people ride without any contact except the weight of the rein, so do not be brainwashed into believing that you must hang on tight to the reins all the time. The heavier your hand, the heavier the pony and the cruder the control; the more you ride with your legs and seat, the 'lighter in hand' the pony, and the more delicate the control. Aim for your pony to be light in hand, as light as a minnow. He cannot be light if you apply enough pressure to tow a dead shark. Keep this idea in mind and your hands will improve.

Punishment

Far too many ponies get punished too often, and far too few riders understand how punishment works. It is important to grasp that, firstly, punishment is only any use when trying to stop a pony doing something; it cannot teach a new action. For instance, you can stop a pony biting by punishing him, but you cannot teach him to change legs at a canter by punishing him if he does not respond when you ask. Secondly, ponies do not see cause and effect in the same way that we do. In order for them to understand that a certain action may lead to trouble and pain, the punishment must come as the action is being done, not some time after. When a pony bites you, it is no use clutching your arm, swearing and examining the damage before hitting back. The pony will make no connection with his biting and being hit, but will simply think you have gone mad. It is not only cruel and useless to give a pony a hiding too long after he has misbehaved; it is also dangerous, for the pony will start disliking this lunatic and may start attacking you. This misuse of punishment is what makes ponies vicious, sullen and mean.

This does not mean that you cannot discipline your pony when he is bad-mannered, but that, if you do, you must do so like other ponies, quickly and honestly. When a youngster playfully bites an old mare's bottom, she will instantly kick him. If she misses, she will not run after him later in order to 'teach him a lesson'; but she will keep an eye on him so that if he tries again she will be ready. Be like a pony: that is what they understand.

Praise
Praise your pony when he pleases you – not before in the hope that he will, nor long afterwards, but at the time. Ponies like the good feeling that comes over you when you praise them and will work hard for it.

Consistency
Try to make sure that you always appear to be the same person to your pony. If you are grumpy, do not take it out on him; if you decide to change your ways, do not expect him to change overnight too. He will get confused if you are sloppy one day and act like a dressage rider the next. This does not mean that you cannot do different things with him, but that, whatever you do, you should always have the same standard of manners and demands. If you want to change, do it gradually.

19 Road Safety

Nowadays in Britain it is rare to ride without going on roads at all. However, ponies and traffic do not mix well. Even if your pony is completely traffic-proof, many drivers are complete idiots. They drive their cars into trees and each other as well as into ponies and many of them have no idea of what frightens a pony. Well-meaning drivers creep soundlessly up to your tail before letting out a blast on the horn. A few shout and whoop at the sight of horses. Rattling trailers covered in loose tarpaulin alarm even the quietest animal. Roads are never predictable, so you must ride with great care.

If you have to ride on roads, remember the following:

Keep to the left, the same side as the traffic, and using any grass verge. However, do not cram yourself into the gutter so that you invite drivers to ignore you. If there is a wide verge on the right but none on the left, you can ride on the right, but your pony is more likely to be upset by the traffic coming towards him. In very narrow lanes, where there is only just room for a car to pass, it is better to ride slowly down the middle so that traffic has to slow or even stop. Otherwise you may find that if you creep along the hedge, people unused to ponies may try to go past far too fast and hit your stirrup with the wing mirror.

Do not gallop on grass verges, however wide the verge and however sensible your pony. Never gallop down the central grass strip of a narrow lane. Verges are often covered in broken bottles and other junk, and a galloping pony is more likely to take fright than one that is walking or trotting.

Always keep your pony well under control, with your reins shorter than usual.

If you are in any doubt about your pony's safety on the road, get off and lead him. You should be on his right, between him and the traffic, staying close to him so he feels protected and talking calmly to him. If he tries to see what is coming from behind he will then turn his hindquarters into the side, not into the traffic. Similarly, when riding you can have the pony's head turned slightly to the right to check behind him, but never to the left.

If in doubt, ask a driver to slow down by holding your hand up, palm forward. Lorry drivers, for instance, will always slow down or stop if you ask them, but usually think that a pony is quiet to pass unless you show that he (or you) is nervous.

Always thank any drivers who slow down, even if you have not asked, so that they may continue to be considerate towards riders.

Do not trot downhill, for tarmac is slippery. Never canter on tarmac. Do not trot fast on a hard surface for long distances, especially if the pony is young or unfit, for the banging will damage his legs. Trotting uphill makes a horse fit, especially if you do a slow sitting trot, leaning back slightly.

Walk round blind corners.

You will find that your pony prefers to trot past things that frighten him, like roadworks and flags, once he has had a look at them and realizes he must go past. Make sure the road ahead and behind is clear, for he may swing out to the opposite side of the road. Make sure, too, that you are well in control and do not let a trot become a mad dash. If in doubt, get off and lead.

Stop at crossroads and zebra crossings. Pavements are for walkers, not horses. Do not frighten pedestrians by riding too close to them.

Do not get caught at the front of a line of traffic waiting for a train to pass at a level crossing. Most ponies get very frightened by trains passing close.

Hand Signals *(Figure 26)*

Put both your reins in one hand (usually the left).

I am turning right Right arm straight out from the shoulder.

I am turning left Left arm out.

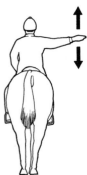

I am stopping Right arm straight out and moved slowly down and up several times if needed.

158

Please slow down (car approaching from behind)   Right arm
out at 45° and moved down and up.

Please slow down or stop (car approaching from ahead)
Right hand up, level with the shoulder, palm forward. Hold it there
until the driver slows.

Please overtake   Right arm out at 45° and make circles clockwise.

Thank you Touch the brim of your hat.

When riding in company on the road, go in pairs, side by side, taking up as much space as a car and keeping two lengths between each pony lest they kick or play up. Keep the boldest ponies front and back. However, if you are doubtful about one of the party, for instance, a small child or a beginner, put her pony on a leading rein on the inside of a sensible pony; lead short, with the led pony's head level with your knee. When crossing another road, come together in a bunch before starting to cross, while the leader stops the traffic. Ride at the pace the slowest can manage comfortably.

If you know you may have to ride in the dusk or in the dark, get reflective bands and foot-straps from a bicycle shop and take great care. A head torch is a good investment.

In winter, never set foot on ice.

20 Having a Useful Pony

For thousands of years nobody much thought of riding ponies around just for the fun of it. Ponies were there to be used: for pulling loads, carts, logs, narrow boats, and ploughs; for getting from A to B, in shafts or under saddle; for hunting, where their keener eye and ear are appreciated; for shepherding and droving, which they learn to do almost by themselves; and for carrying other loads. Nowadays in Britain most ponies are seldom used for anything but pleasure, and they seem to make a good deal of work for their owners, who have never taught them to do anything useful.

Any riding pony should be able to be tied up without fretting, cross water, enter a trailer, be shod, jump small jumps, step over difficult obstacles, be ridden one-handed, allow the rider to open gates without dismounting, and carry parcels, bags, buckets and haynets, be traffic-proof, and come when called. All these are a matter of the rider having patience and determination. Life becomes easier and more fun if your pony will also ground-tie (that is, stand still when the reins are dropped to the ground, as most Western horses do), carry loads of hay and feed, carry a pack saddle, wear fancy dress, settle quickly with new companions and in new places, walk up and down steps or even through houses, be tethered overnight or longer, and carry two or three children: in short, be adaptable. Highly useful ponies will also pull sledges, harrows or anything else in chains, drive in shafts, work sheep and cattle and understand new problems quickly. All these abilities are well within the reach of most ordinary ponies (highly bred horses are rather less useful). However, if you never ask a pony to try he will never learn. Ponies that have many skills learn the

Tethered pony, half-Arab gelding, looks well on his varied diet. He is so aware of his chain that he can safely lie down and roll. A pony on a tether is, however, subject to abuse: he may have no shelter or water, soon runs out of food (he needs moving every day at least), and could be teased by hooligans.

This pony has very good legs and feet, with strong, well-formed joints next ones more easily, so it is up to you to find challenges and interesting problems.

When you are asking a pony to learn something new, make sure you are not in a hurry. Ponies like to be able to take a good look, smell at and nuzzle at new things. They get suspicious if you try to rush them, and if you give up without doing what you wanted they get the habit of refusing. Try to make it obvious what you want to do. This means you may have to think out how to tackle the problem in advance. If it means going somewhere odd or carrying something strange, show the pony you would not mind yourself. She should find it easy to do the right thing and impossible to do anything else. Keep her attention on the problem and do not let her suggest easier ways out. Always praise any attempt she makes, even if she backs out afterwards. If you fail, do not punish her but go on trying until you succeed.

Many new problems have to split up into smaller parts, because ponies tend to panic if they have to cope with too many new ideas at once. Nobody would put an untrained pony straight into a trap, but the training necessary is really a matter of getting her used to each new idea in turn, one at a time: being controlled from behind, pulling things that stop when she does (logs, etc.), feeling the shafts along her sides, hearing the trap, and so on.

Two points of safety: first, if a pony gets legs tangled in ropes he will kick and rope-burn himself. When teaching a pony to tether or haul loads it is best to use chains (the pony can also hear where they are, which helps), but very fat ropes, like ships' ropes, will do. Second, ponies cannot see wire well. If you are asking a pony to step near wire, move it or make it obvious by putting your saddle, numnah or clothes over it.

When using any new equipment, show it to the pony first, patting it, jingling anything that moves, carrying it about in front of him in a way that shows it doesn't worry you at all. He will probably want to smell it.

Ground-Tying

Do not use your reins at first or he'll break them and bruise his mouth. Start by dropping the lead rope of a halter on the ground, saying 'stand'. If he starts to move, jerk the lead rope downwards as if he is tied to something on the ground. When he stands for a second or two, take a couple of steps away. If he moves, raise your hand sharply and cry 'no!'. Do not expect too much at first, and reward him even if he stands for only a short while. Keep going and be firm. He will take weeks to learn to stand reliably. Ground-tie when grooming, saddling or just standing about.

Tethering

Start with a fairly short length of chain or ships' rope or hold the end of a longer length while he grazes. Do not leave him alone at first as he will certainly get into a muddle a few times. When he does, call 'whoa' calmly and untangle him slowly. Try to get him to understand that, when in difficulty, the thing to do is stop still, not panic. As he gets used to the idea you will see him start to sidestep to avoid the chain.

When you first leave him alone on the tether, let it be for no longer than an hour. It will take him that long to fill his stomach, after that he may get bored. Eventually you should tether from a neck strap, not the halter. Experienced ponies can live tethered for years, rolling and lying down in perfect safety, so aware are they of the chain.

Carrying Loads

Always show the pony the load first, carrying it yourself so he understands that any noise it might make is not threatening. Put it on his back, turning his head so he can see it. Make sure he is relaxed before moving off. If he panics and bucks it off, do not give up; give him time to relax and start again. Whenever he starts to tense up, stop him and soothe him.

Bales of hay can be carried two at a time if tied together at one end and slung over the pony's back. Remember that the pony will forget how high and wide the load is, so take care going through gates or he will be surprised when the load snags.

The pad from an old cart harness, the type with a metalled groove, makes a useful pack saddle for slow work. If you are going longer

164

A useful pony carries his own food and ground-ties reliably. The bales are tied together at the top and slung over his back; he is so unconcerned he is resting one back leg. This pony has exceptionally good legs. He is very long from hip to hock, which gives him great speed, like a greyhound; his long strong pasterns give great spring. He never wears a bit and this bridle is home-made from plaited cord; one rein can be unclipped from the ring at his chin so he can be tied

distances or camping, you will have to buy or make a proper pack saddle (see chapter 27). If the packs are well balanced and properly lashed on (quite an art), the pony can gallop and jump as well as a ridden pony.

Pulling Loads

If your pony is quiet and does not mind things behind him, you can start this yourself, but if he is nervous or kicks, leave it to a professional. Use a pad or surcingle and collar or breastband. First, have someone lead the pony while you drive him from behind with two

Learning to sidestep while turning in chains. The pony has to leave the load where it is and move himself round it. The breastband is rigged from a girth tied to the saddle: he could not pull much weight like this. His head is tipped up so he can see his hocks, and his ears show that he is concentrating on what is happening behind him.

He is lashing his tail slightly because he finds this new task difficult

long reins. Allow these to droop occasionally so he gets used to them touching his back legs. Show the pony the chains, which should be twice his length. After dragging them along yourself start to drive him while you drag them. Show him that the noise stops when he does. Now attach the chains to the hames on the collar, or to the point where the breastband meets the pad and lead him along so that the chains drag on the ground behind him. He should realize that whenever things go wrong, for instance if he treads on one of the chains or steps over it while turning round, stopping is the answer rather than running away. He must be thoroughly used to dragging the chains before you try attaching a load.

166

Next, take a piece of wood 2–3 feet long and drag it alongside, then tie it between the chains behind him to act as a spacer. Once he is used to this you can attach your load to this bar but be sure you show it to him first. Use light loads to begin with and only gradually increase them.

Take care when going round corners or turning round, for the chains will come tight against his legs. The right way to turn is to leave the load where it is and to make him sidestep to face the new direction before setting off again.

Do not let him go too fast. This is usually a sign of nervousness and he may speed up too much. You may need two people, one each side, at first, to keep him straight and, more difficult, stop him straight.

Once he is well used to hauling, your pony can pull one section of a chain harrow round your field to spread manure and clear foggage (long old grass). A makeshift harrow can be made from a heavy gate laid on blackthorn bushes. If you try pulling a sledge, do realize that you need someone behind as a brake to stop it overtaking the pony downhill if the surface is hard and slippy.

Driving

It is much riskier teaching a pony to pull in shafts: seek professional help. If you have bought a pony advertised as 'ride and drive', you would be wise to take expert advice the first time you try driving. If a driven pony runs away he usually does not stop until he hits something or rolls the cart. However, when hauling loads you are at the pony's head, with more control and more reassurance; moreover he is unlikely to hurt himself in chains, especially if you take his training slowly and methodically.

21 Improving Control: Elementary Schooling

By 'schooling' we mean exercising the pony in such a way that we teach her to collect herself: to carry herself better, make crisper changes of pace, and respond more precisely to the aids. In fact, a good rider never stops schooling his horse, even when hacking. Hacking does not mean riding carelessly: the thinking rider does not allow his horse to slop along, but uses features of the landscape, like trees, banks and gates, as opportunities to supple and balance her. However, for better concentration of the less disciplined pony and rider, schooling usually takes place in a flat school or manège.

It is better for your pony if you do not try to school her in her own field. If you have no alternative, then fence off a section to make a schooling area. If you bed your pony on peat or wood shavings you will find that the used bedding helps to stop your school turning into a mud slick.

Begin a schooling session by trotting in a large circle to warm the pony up; warm yourself up with some exercises too. At first leave your reins fairly loose so she stretches her neck and spine. Encourage her to do this, and use your seat, back and legs to push forwards so her hindquarters are really working. Aim at free forward movement, which is the first and most important purpose in riding. Get her to do a long, swinging trot rather than a hasty choppy one. It is only when her back is swinging and elastic that she uses her hindquarters fully. In order to help keep a rhythm, find a song of the right tempo and keep singing it. As she extends her pace she will stretch her neck; increasingly her hocks will come farther underneath her at each step, so that she starts carrying herself with her back legs rather than just pushing herself forward with them. As this happens you will find it becomes increasingly easy to steer her with your legs only.

When you have been working for five or ten minutes allow her to walk, relaxed, before starting again. When you have picked up this good trot again, start working in a figure 8 or making L turns unexpectedly. If her hindquarters have truly developed impulsion you will find that you are hurtling into these bends without sufficient control, because there is too much push from behind. At this point the pony is asking to be collected. Pick up your rein slightly without allowing her hindquarters to stop working. Do not lose the rhythm or the elastic energy you have developed. You will find that the pony's head will come up slightly, that she tucks her nose in a little, and that her back shortens and lifts. Maintain the contact with her mouth that is necessary to control her enough to make your manoeuvres, but keep it light, as light as possible.

If you find it difficult to feel these changes, try making quick changes of pace from walk to trot and back again – say, ten paces of each. When making a crisp transition the pony collects herself and stays collected for two or three paces before relaxing into her previous sloppy state. You can feel the difference in her back at this time: the ligament that runs from her poll to her dock contracts so that her hindquarters come under her, her back rises, her neck arches and her nose tucks in. Try to maintain the impulsion she generates at the transition, extending it so she keeps it up for three, then four, then ten paces before asking for the reverse transition. You will feel the changes in her back even better if you work bareback.

Another exercise that makes a pony collect himself is the half halt. This is exactly what it sounds like: ask the pony to stop, by driving him forward with your seat on to your unyielding hand, but before he has quite stopped, ask him to walk forward briskly.

You can also feel a pony's back working if you ride bareback uphill. If you watch another pony going uphill you will see how much he gets his hocks under him to generate energy better. Another simple exercise which makes the pony collect himself is trotting in and out of barrels placed at random around the arena.

During collection, then, the pony generates energy, or impulsion, from behind, but you do not allow it to flow away in front. In this way we can compare the pony's back to a whippy stick, which is pushed forward with one hand but held back at the other end by another

hand. The bent stick stores a good deal of energy: if it is suddenly released with the front hand it springs forward. It is this contained energy that makes riding a collected horse such a delight, for he is ready and able immediately to make any movement you want. On a relaxed pony you cannot even go from a walk to a trot without a stage of shuffling while he shortens his back.

Being 'On the Bit'

The commonest, almost universal fault in schooling is to try to collect a pony from in front by hauling her upwards and backwards with your hands. Clearly this does not produce the same result at all. Whereas in true collection the pony lowers her hindquarters and raises her forehand, so that the seesaw effect mentioned earlier results in lightness in front, in this false collection the forequarters cannot be raised since the rein cannot make the hindquarters lower. However, there is a common misunderstanding of the idea 'on the bit' which

Above left: Pulling on the reins does not collect the horse: instead he stiffens his jaw and neck, resisting the bit. His back is lowered and he moves in an ugly, uncontrolled manner.

Above: When the rider uses her legs and seat to drive him on, the horse yields to the bit, arching his neck, raising his back and using his hind legs more.

This rider is very round-shouldered, both on and off the horse, and her hunched position, with hands too far forward, tends to tip the horse's weight forward and make him heavy in front

leads to some false conclusions and hence this false attempt at collection.

Being 'on the bit' means that the pony accepts the bit and does not try to avoid it by tipping her head up and back ('above the bit') or by tucking her nose in to her chest ('behind the bit'). It does not mean that she leans on the bit, which is what most ponies will do if encouraged by a dead hand. For most ponies it is easier to balance by leaning heavily on the rider's hand rather than rebalancing themselves; if the rider misunderstands the lightness that the right contact

This pretty three-quarter Arab palamino, newly bought, is afraid of her mouth being hurt. Although Ceri has the reins loose the pony looks frightened and miserable. In order to escape the bit she raises her head, hollows her back and moves in an ugly, stilted manner. When she hots up she becomes totally unmanageable, running away, with her head straight up. This uncomfortable, upset look is typical of many Arab ponies

with the pony's mouth implies, he will accept this weight. Look at the difference in style between classical dressage as practised by the Spanish Riding School or the Saumur school, and the heavier Germanic type of dressage, and you will see that lightness is all too often lost even at the highest level. However, this advanced training is beyond the scope of this book. But the novice does better to keep his mind on the ideas of impulsion, that thrust of energy from behind, and lightness in hand, rather than worrying about contact and being on the bit, for these almost inevitably follow.

172

Two minutes later, in a hackamore for the first time ever, the pony is much happier. Her back has come up and her hocks come further under her, while she trots out more freely and confidently. This borrowed hackamore is too loose and comes dangerously low on the pony's nose. Ceri will do better to lengthen her stirrups and keep her lower leg further back, but as she gains confidence in being able to control her new, spirited pony she will lose that tense look

One other problem concerns Arab ponies in particular. Remembering the whippy stick, we can see that the bend in it can curve upwards or downwards. If a pony bends his back downwards, his hind legs go out behind him, his neck dips instead of arching, and his nose rises and sticks out (above the bit). This way of going is often seen in Arabs, which tend to dislike a heavy hand, so that any attempt at false collection from in front is instantly shown up. Many people overcome this problem with mechanical devices which do bring the pony's head down but also destroy that lovely elegance so typical of the breed. (Watch carefully at shows and you will see Arab ponies in the 'correct' shape but totally lacking the free, floating action so characteristic of the breed.) With such a pony it is important rather to develop impulsion by asking for energetic, extended paces before any attempt at collection is made, for in an extended pace the neck stretches down and forward instead of tipping backwards. Do a lot of work over cavaletti (see chapter 22) and when schooling leave the odd pole around the school and the pony will soon hold his head more reasonably. Even then it is important to keep in mind that the point of having a well-schooled pony is that he is pleasant to ride and responds quickly and willingly to the aids, rather than that his silhouette conforms to a preconceived notion.

Suppling

Most elementary schoolwork is done at the trot; a pony cannot canter comfortably in a small space until he has grasped some idea of collecting himself. Suppleness is also important. Many ponies are stiffer on one side than the other (generally the left) and so find it more difficult to canter leading on the opposite leg. When cantering in a circle, the pony should always lead with the inside leg. If you are already trotting in a circle the pony will probably pick up that lead, but the aids for cantering on the left leg are: left rein direct, right rein indirect, left leg on the girth to maintain impulsion, right leg sharply behind the girth together with a strong push from your seat as you sit down.

If you find it impossible to get your pony to canter on the right (i.e. off) leg even when circling to the right, it will be because he is stiff on that side. It is no use getting annoyed with him or thinking him obstinate, for he will probably get worse until he hates you even asking. Try asking him to canter on a lunge rein until he does it easily. If he fails, you will need to supple him, either by using difficult natural situations – rough ground, banks, weaving your way in and out of trees – or by practising suppling movements. The simplest is the shoulder-in. Here the pony walks forward but is bent to one side, so that his back feet no longer follow his front ones. The body describes a bend as if the pony were moving in a circle. For a right shoulder-in, turn the forehand with your hands as for a circle, but ask him to go

174

straight forwards with your legs. You will have to push hard with your right leg; you may have to slide the left leg back to prevent his hindquarters swinging out. The pony is likely to resist and get bothered because he does not understand what you are asking. Usually a shoulder-in is done along the straight side of a manège with the shoulder turned in to the centre, but it is often easier, especially with an older pony who thinks you have got confused, to do it along a lane or path where it is obvious that he must go forward. Do not ask for too much bend at first; be pleased if he even tries and only increase your demands gradually. After all, you are deliberately asking him for a movement you know he will find difficult.

When you have mastered work in large circles, reduce your speed and work in small ones; then work in straight lines. You will find it more difficult than you suppose to get the pony moving absolutely straight. In any session, start with the circles and figure 8s to supple him before going straight.

Do not sicken your pony with too much school work. Work through the exercises you have mastered before trying anything new, and be sure to praise and reward where this is due.

You will not be able to improve your pony by schooling him unless you pay great attention to your own riding. Make sure you are not leaning forward and that you use your seat as well as your legs to gain impulsion. Make sure, too, that you ride with equal care when out hacking or the whole point will be lost.

22 Jumping

Unless he has been thoroughly put off, any pony will jump at least the height of his front legs. For the novice rider the main problem with jumping is avoiding jerking at the reins in mid-jump, for this will instantly put the pony off.

If you ride with a long stirrup, take the leathers up two holes and practise your jumping position by scrambling up banks and steep slopes. Lean right forward, hands well up the pony's neck, without hauling at his mouth or letting your legs slip back. You will be going at about the same angle when jumping, so this slower work will help you develop your position. Practise also standing in the stirrups while trotting and cantering. You need a firm knee grip when jumping, and this will help develop it. When you have mastered these two exercises you can start trotting over poles on the ground and cavaletti (poles raised 8 inches or so above the ground).

Cavaletti and jumps need to be wide and solid. You will need four or five poles each 10 feet long and 6 inches in diameter. Cavaletti proper have their ends resting on crosses, but you can balance your poles on bricks, blocks or cans. First, measure the length of your pony's stride while trotting. You can do this by trotting him over mud or sand; you can also get a good guess at it by running alongside him while he trots, matching your step to his. It is important to get this length right as you need to space your poles at this distance or he cannot trot over them. Again, you need to make it easy for him to do the right thing.

Set four or five poles, evenly spaced at this length, on the ground to begin with. You will find it easier to have one end against a fence. Allow the pony to examine them and walk over them before trotting at them. As you approach your reins should be slightly shorter than usual and your hands slightly in front of their normal position. The pony will almost certainly want to slow to a walk immediately in front of the poles, so keep his speed up with your legs. As you go over the poles let your hands give forwards to allow him to stretch his neck without pulling at the bit, and lean forward. His trot will be bouncier than usual. If you are unbalanced by this, grasp the mane halfway up the neck with both hands or use a neckstrap to steady yourself. It is very important that you do not jolt his mouth as he bounces.

Gradually raise the height of your cavaletti to a foot or so. When you and the pony have mastered these you are ready to jump.

Good jumping seat. The rider's light, sensitive hands allow the horse freedom to stretch her neck without dragging at the bit; his weight goes forward with hers and his lower leg is firm

177

Building Jumps

Make your first jumps small, wide and solid. The easiest first jumps are made of two crossed poles, with one end of each pole resting on a block and the other on the ground so the jump is lowest in the middle. You can start by trotting over this, too, then try increasing your speed. Do not start to canter a long way away from the jump; you should aim to canter for only the last three strides, increasing your speed all the time and giving an extra push with your legs as you take off. You are almost bound to get left behind at first, so be sure to use the mane or neckstrap to make sure you do not hurt his mouth.

If there is a track or path you can build small jumps across you will find the pony almost certainly jumps them more readily than in a field. Gateways or gaps in walls also make obvious places for jumps. Until you really have the feel of the rhythm, make it easier for both of you by placing your jumps so they are hard to avoid. Ponies jump better going towards home.

By far the best place for both you and the pony to learn is in a jumping lane. This is a fenced corridor across which jumps are built so there is no avoiding them. The pony is first made to jump free, by letting her go at one end and rattling a bucket of food at the other. When she jumps confidently, start riding her. You do not really need reins in a jumping lane; you can learn to jump with folded arms, but if you want to practise your hand position you can ride in a headcollar.

Do not be too ambitious at first. In jumping, nothing succeeds like success. The more small jumps you jump faultlessly the more likely you are to clear bigger ones; the more your pony runs out or refuses the better she learns to avoid jumping.

Ponies get sick of jumping quite quickly, so do not go on and on clearing the same jump, no matter how much fun it seems to you. Change your jumps often.

The most difficult jumps are single bars: the pony cannot easily tell how far away they are unless you put a ground pole in front. This should be as far from the jump as the jump is high. Even then it is best to put another bar between the two, making a spread, which looks more solid. Make brush jumps from piles of branches. If you are short of stout poles, car tyres threaded through or rested against a pole make it more solid. Petrol cans, doors (at an angle, not upright), mattresses and old feed sacks stuffed with paper make good jump

good jumps

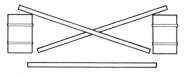

crossed poles with ground pole in front

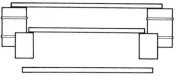

3-bar spread

threaded car tyres

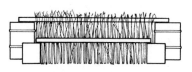

sticks and poles, looking solid

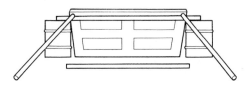

leaning door with ground pole and wings

bad jumps

pole too flimsy   jump too narrow
no ground line   no solidity

flimsy sticks higher in middle

upright door
no ground line: hard for pony to judge

Figure 27 Jumps

179

material. You can also make interesting and unusual jumps by raiding your local rubbish dump and applying bright paint. Keep them low, solid and broad.

Building Courses

When trying a series of jumps, do not assume that if the pony jumps the first one he will automatically jump the second. After the first jump you will find that he is going a good deal faster than before and will simply career off with you unless you regain control. Steady him, to a trot if necessary, and approach the second jump as if it were completely separate. If your pony gets overexcited by jumping several jumps, arrange them in a circle instead of a straight line.

If the pony keeps running out, make your jumps wider. Build wings that funnel him into the jump, and make jumps that sag in the middle so it is actually easier for him to jump them than to run out. It does not matter if your jump is 20 feet wide and 1 foot high. The point is to jump it successfully and to be able to reward your pony.

Problems

If the pony keeps refusing, your jumps may be too high or he may be afraid of what you will do. Gain his confidence by work over very low jumps, by lunging him without a rider, then by being lunged on him without reins. Always reward him when he jumps, however small the jump, and you will find he improves. However, he may be refusing because you are not using your legs enough on the approach.

It may be months before a pony becomes confident enough to jump higher with you (no matter what she is like with anyone else). As with people, ponies that are pushed unsympathetically into something that frightens them grow to hate what they are doing. Jumping is a nervy, exciting affair for both rider and pony. A few ponies, like some people, seem to revel in the thrill of it; most, if their experience of jumping is good, come to enjoy moderate jumps; and some, either through bad experiences or deep-rooted nervousness, take a dim view of it. Whatever the pony's temperament, jumping does require nerve, and ponies are easily put off by being beaten, shouted at, overjumped or overfaced. Always reward a pony, even if only with a pat or a word of praise, every time he jumps.

Preparing for Competitions

If you and your pony enjoy jumping and seem to be good at it, so that you think of competing, take yourselves to a good instructor for a few training sessions. Jumping is so much a question of feeling rhythm and calculating distances that it is difficult to become good at it by reading books. There are numerous faults that you can get away with over small fences, but that spell doom over larger ones: rushing fences, taking off too close, lack of impulsion, poor rhythm and so on. If you correct these mistakes early you are far more assured of success. A half-hour lesson that leaves you with homework for weeks is a better investment than another book or a wasted entry fee.

The pony will also benefit from jumping in a different place. In strange places ponies often seem to forget all they have learned, so endless jumping at home does not necessarily improve a pony in competition. Instead, arrange sessions at different places and keep ringing the changes so she does not get complacent. Make sure that at least half your jumps are small, strange ones, and do not jump her more than twice a week including competitions.

Take care not to spoil a good pony by overdoing it. If she starts refusing in competitions where she did not before, it is a sign that she has had enough for now. Carrying on usually makes matters worse. Lay off for a few months or change the kind of competition entirely.

After a jumping session, look after your pony's legs. Cool them by hosing or with cold-water bandages if you think there is a chance of a strain.

23 Travelling and Trekking

Transporting Your Pony

Ponies do not like to be cooped up in small, dark, rattling boxes. Travelling frightens them unless they are well used to it. As well as mental strain, they also suffer from physical strain during travelling. Scientific research has shown that these strains are greatly reduced if the pony travels facing the rear, for the movement disturbs and frightens her less. If you have a front-loading trailer or one large enough for her to turn round in, always allow her to face the rear. She will do this herself if you leave her loose, which is quite safe. However, do not leave the pony untied if she cannot turn round, for she may try to do so and panic or hurt herself.

If you are thinking of buying a trailer, get one that allows the pony to face the rear. If you use a cattle or sheep trailer, be sure to put a bar above the ramp so she cannot climb out. In a large cattle wagon, put the pony in sideways and use a barricade to keep her in position, rather than leaving her loose in a huge space. A sheep trailer is too small for anything larger than a very small pony.

It is best to bandage your pony's legs or use travelling boots. Bandages should be well padded and reach from the coronet to the knee; the fastenings must be reliable. A tail bandage covers the upper part of the tail only and should not be too tight for fear of restricting the circulation in the dock.

Do not travel a pony bridled or saddled. You may need to rug him, for many boxes and trailers are draughty. In cold weather on a long journey, use several rugs and stop every hour or so to see he is not chilled. Overheating may be a problem in hot weather.

If your pony has had no travelling experience, prepare him well by feeding him on the ramp and then in the trailer for several days beforehand. He will be helped by being accompanied by a pony that is a seasoned traveller.

Make sure that everything is ready before you load the pony, especially if he is not used to travelling. Aim to drive away as soon as the ramp is up, for he is more likely to get agitated in a stationary trailer than in a moving one, as his worry about the movement keeps him quiet. Similarly, try to arrange that you stop only to check him, briefly. Have the vehicle full of fuel, and take sandwiches and a flask for yourself. In hot weather a trailer becomes very stuffy while standing still, so make any stops short even if your pony does not mind travelling.

When loading, remember the following: a pony will enter a large box more easily than a small one, a dirty box more easily than a clean one, a light one rather than a dark one, a gently sloping ramp rather than a steep one. If he can smell that horses have been in before, feel that the ramp is solid and see that you are not afraid of being inside it will help. Open the jockey door if there is one. Ponies hate to be rushed over loading: take your time and keep calm, even if you are late. Nothing makes a pony more suspicious than being rushed by an agitated person.

Lead the pony in confidently. If he does not follow, go in yourself and try to bribe him. Be patient. Many ponies will load perfectly well after thinking about it for five minutes. If he refuses, have someone come quietly behind him. Do not hit him, shout or wave things.

If he still refuses, have two helpers hold hands under his tail, round his buttocks; he cannot kick them if they are standing close to his flanks. With only one helper, tie a rope to one side of the trailer level with his buttocks, run it round them to the other side, and pull. You can also try to 'walk' him in by picking up each foot in turn and putting it on the ramp, while keeping up pressure from behind and in front. This usually works, but watch out in case he suddenly rushes backwards down the ramp.

If you are alone with a horse that is difficult to load, you will need a rope about 30 feet long without knots in it. Run this from the pony's headcollar through the tethering ring at the front of the trailer, back down his side, round his buttocks, if possible round a stanchion or through a ventilation hole at the same height, and back to you. By

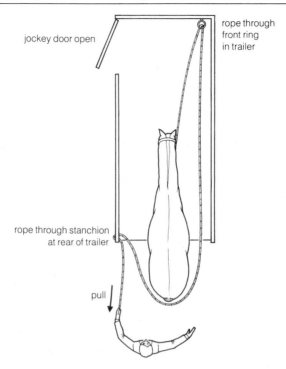

jockey door open

rope through
front ring
in trailer

rope through stanchion
at rear of trailer

pull

Figure 28 Rope system for difficult loader

pulling it you not only pull his head forward but also push his hindquarters forward. As he moves up the ramp, take up the slack and refuse to let him move back. You can usually manage to hold him with one hand and pat his rump or lift his feet with the other. If you have any doubts about loading, rig up this rope even before your first attempt, so that he does not refuse to load and then keep playing up.

Many ponies walk in without fuss but try to back out immediately. Have someone behind to fasten the buttock strap or raise the ramp as quickly as possible.

It is dangerous to frighten a horse into a box because he may rear as he reaches the top of the ramp, hit his head on the back of the roof and kill himself. It is also dangerous to blindfold him (a suggestion often made because it often works). Unless the box is huge he can easily walk off the edge of the ramp or panic himself by bumping against the sides or end of the box.

In a double trailer, the passenger-side stall away from incoming

184

traffic, is the less frightening one. Travel a single pony, or the more nervous of the two, on that side.

When driving, imagine you have a glass of water on the top of your head. Do not brake suddenly or corner fast. When approaching a junction or traffic lights, slow down well in advance and try not to stop completely, for any stop, however gentle, is a strain on the pony.

A long journey is a strain to a pony and she must be allowed time to recover peacefully. Nervous ponies sweat badly, and should be dried and reassured after arrival.

Do not travel in a trailer with your pony; you cannot communicate with the driver if anything goes wrong, and it is illegal. If you feel the pony will be nervous, stop briefly to check and reassure her, and call to her out of the window as you travel.

When unloading, untie the pony's head before or as you undo the buttock strap, for he may try to run backwards as soon as the strap is unclipped. If he refuses to back out, lay the lead rope over his neck and let go of him. He may want to put his head down or turn it to see behind him. Give him time before trying to persuade him. Stand beside the ramp if it has no sides, so he does not step off it. Some ponies are liable to come out of a trailer in a rush and resent any attempt to slow them down.

Trekking

Horses were, after all, the major means of travelling before engines and none is more enjoyable, given a good route, the right gear, a good pony and a bit of luck with the weather.

A pony that does not tether is a hindrance on a journey, so make sure yours is well trained. If you have two ponies you will only have to tether one. A fit pony will go up to 40 miles a day if well fed, but for pleasure do not reckon on more than 15–20 miles a day. At this rate she will need a feed each day but will not collapse if she misses the odd one. A fit pony that is used to travelling will cope on good grass alone; a seasoned traveller wastes no time in fretting and is quick to take any opportunity to eat.

Planning

When planning your journey, try not to be too rigid. If the pony casts a shoe, gets loose, or seems tired; if the bridleway is impassable (they are not guaranteed in good order) or you get lost; or if the weather turns foul or you meet a stallion on the hill, you may find yourself unexpectedly benighted. So do not plan a journey that absolutely requires you to be in a certain place at a certain time. You will need to make arrangements for overnight grazing and extra feeds, but you must also make sure you can camp out on the spot if necessary.

Bridleways groups and local riding clubs will be of great help when planning a route, but your arrangements will vary with the area. In the lowlands you will certainly want to arrange overnight stops beforehand, but in most well-ridden areas you are more likely to find bridleways open and information easy to get. In mountain country you can generally camp above the mountain wall without any problem, but you are more likely to find bridleways blocked (especially by the Forestry Commission or the Economic Forestry Group), overgrown or impassable due to bogs after heavy rain.

Equipment

Absolute essentials are: old, well-fitting, comfortable tack; good, detailed maps; a thick saddle blanket; a tether rope or chain; penknife, string, needle and strong thread. A saddle with D rings (army saddles are best) is really useful, as are saddle bags, a compass for high country, waterproofs, a piece of tarpaulin to keep your blanket dry, a space blanket (emergency bivouac blanket, heat-proof and very light) and a billycan. Do not carry a rucksack: they make trotting and cantering almost impossible. Make a long roll of your gear, long enough to hang down each side of the pony, and lash it tightly over the pommel or behind the saddle, making sure it rests on thick blanket rather than on the pony's skin if you have no saddlebags.

If you intend to camp you will find it easiest to take a packpony: one can carry enough for three people and after a while you will find that she does not need leading except on roads. Pack saddles are difficult to get but a good saddler or woodworker will be able to make one (see chapter 27). Packs must be balanced carefully or the saddle will rub. Lash your gear on firmly, making sure it will not flop up and down.

Daily regime

Each morning, feed first thing and check carefully for any signs of strain or chafing (hot or irritable skin). Travel for two or three hours only before stopping. At each stop, unsaddle the pony immediately and tether him on good grazing for an hour and a half. In this time he will fill his belly and get a good rest. In this way you can make three stages on a long day and still arrive unjaded. If you push your pony for longer than that you will find that after a week he will be exhausted and thin.

Feed again last thing at night. If you have no stabling or grazing for the night you will have to tether, picket or tie the pony. If you are not sure about tethering while you are asleep, leave him as long as possible before tying him, and untie as soon as possible in the morning. To picket, tie a rope as tight as possible at head height between two trees. Tie the pony's lead rope to this with a karabiner (ask at a climbing or outdoor shop), so that he can just reach the ground to graze. He can then walk up and down the length of the picket rope in safety.

Problems

Most parts of Britain are heavily populated and help is seldom far away in an emergency. Remember that dairy farms always have cattle cake if you are desperate for food. However, in high country you need to take care that you do not get into trouble. You must have a sensible and surefooted pony: this is where the survival instinct of the true native pony, which can be rather hampering in other forms of riding, really comes into its own. Particular dangers are getting lost, especially in forestry where maps are not reliable, or in mist; getting into bogs; and finding the way blocked by a fence. Check with local farmers before crossing remote areas. Learn to use a compass; learn to listen to your pony.

In boggy areas always follow paths and do not force the pony on if he feels unsafe. Look for bracken, gorse and heath bedstraw, which are indicators of dry ground. If the pony goes down, throw yourself off immediately and haul his head to one side. Act quickly: even if the pony goes right down you can extricate him by throwing him over on one side and rolling him over so his feet are on firmer ground, but if you are not quick enough he will flounder and dig himself in too far. You will then be in serious danger and must use your wits and anything that comes to hand, including your saddle placed flat, to provide a footing for his front feet. Keep his head up.

If you are absolutely sure of your mapreading you are within your rights to remove a blockage across a bridleway. This includes cutting a fence, though you must always make it stockproof again and inform the local authority Highways Department what you have done and why. Never ask a pony to step over wire without covering it first, using your saddle and blanket.

Be kind to your pony on a long journey. Always allow free access to water; dismount and let him nibble while you stop for a chat; above all, be ready to listen when he complains, and you can keep going for months; be thoughtless, and he will be finished in two days. Most ponies love journeys, and there is nothing like travelling to bring you close to your pony, make him prepared for anything, liven his interest and make you realize what an intelligent creature a pony is.

24 Shows, Gymkhanas and Rallies

Ponies enjoy occasional shows but tend to get sickened by too much competitive work, especially when they are used for little else. Shows are exciting, which means that too many can become a strain. Many a good pony has been ruined by ambition and greed. Part of the problem is that many people become insensitive while competing, thinking only of the prize rather than of the pony.

There are a hundred different forms of competition: do make sure you pick one suitable for your pony and that you know exactly what is required well in advance, to avoid disappointment and embarrassment. For instance, in a riding pony class the judges look for a particular kind of conformation and schooling, not, as might be supposed, a good all-round child's pony. If your pony hasn't that type of looks, go for a performance class like a handy pony competition.

Most serious competitions are run by various national governing bodies which may demand membership before you can enter. These are the British Horse Society, the British Show Jumping Association, the Endurance Horse and Pony Society and the BHS Long-Distance Riding Group. They may demand that you qualify before entering. For in-hand breed classes you may be asked to produce registration papers or be a member of the relevant breed society.

For the novice, though, there are many smaller shows, competitions run by riding centres and riding clubs, and gymkhanas that do not require membership. The easiest jumping classes for the novice are the clear-round competition, where all who succeed get a rosette, and the chase-me-Charlie, a gymkhana event where all competitors follow one another over a single jump that is gradually raised.

Preparing for a Show

When intending to compete, start your training well in advance so that you do not have to do more than a couple of training sessions a week. When you think you are nearly ready, start changing the places in which you practise. Ponies get used to recognizing what is being asked of them from the place they are used to; many appear to forget everything they have learned the first few times they are shown, due to the rider ignoring this 'place effect'. Take your pony to practise in a friend's field or find places while out hacking where you can practise, so he realizes that the place and company do not matter.

A long day takes its toll, so step up your feeding for a couple of days before a show or rally. Make sure your tack is spotless, your clothes in order. When showing in hand, a hacking jacket and trousers are acceptable; you must have shoes you can run in. For a riding class wear a riding jacket, jodhpurs and jodhpur boots or riding boots. Long hair should be tucked into a hairnet under your hat. For a gymkhana be clean and comfortable, in clothes that allow you to jump on and off and run quickly; you should be able to remove and replace your hat quickly too. For rallies, dress sensibly: a rally is not a fashion parade.

You may want to trim or plait your pony for a show. Native ponies are shown with full mane and tail; finer types are generally plaited or have their manes pulled and trimmed. Never cut a pony's mane: the results are always disappointing.

To pull a mane
Take a few strands of long hair, run a metal comb halfway up their length from below so you include only the longest hairs, and pull sharply downwards. A tail is pulled only on the sides of the dock, to trim straggly hairs. However, pulling is a painful business for the pony, and if you regularly brush or comb the pony's mane it will need less pulling.

To plait a mane
Plaiting needs a thin mane. Traditionally seven or nine plaits are made, plus one in front. Divide the mane equally and plait very tight, plaiting in a long thick thread. Roll the plait underneath itself, thread a

190

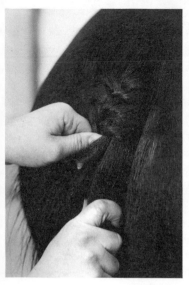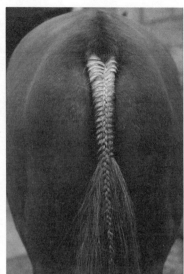

Plaiting a tail and the end result

needle with the plaited-in thread and sew together firmly. Sewn plaits look much neater than ones fastened with elastic bands.

To plait a tail

Do not pull it: you need the long hairs each side of the dock. Take a few of these on each side, starting at the top, and pull them tight to cross each other in the middle. Hold the plait with one hand to keep it tight while bringing in another strand from one side, then the other. Continue for 6 inches or so, finishing with a narrow plait down the middle of the tail. Finish with a loop. Plaiting a tail well takes practice but looks very neat and avoids having to rip the pony's hair out.

Banging

Banging means cutting the tail square just below the hocks. It should not be done to Arab or native ponies, but is suitable for English cob or hunter types. Lift the whole tail up a few inches by putting your arm underneath it: a pony naturally carries his tail higher when moving than when you are fiddling with it (see cover photograph). A banged

191

tail looks better if you plait the top and bandage it to keep it neat. Dampen the tail before bandaging (setting lotion helps) and do not bandage too tight. Leave the bandage on overnight, removing it the last moment before entering the ring.

A wavy tail, as seen on some ponies, is enhanced by washing it a day or two before, whirling the end below the dock to spin-dry it and plaiting tight, including one leg of a pair of tights in the plait. Double the plait under, put it into the other leg of the tights and tie it up firmly. When undone, this produces a pretty effect. Again, setting lotion helps.

Grooming should be extra thorough for a week before the show. Strapping will help make the pony glow. Avoid washing if you can. Do not clip the whiskers: it is cruel and unnecessary.

The night before the show, bring your pony in to a spotless box if possible, or he will surely lie in the dirtiest part of the field. Sort out tack. Emergency tack: a spare pair of reins, a needle and thread, safety pins, shoelaces (very handy).

Morning of show: get up early, feed, plait and groom before breakfast. Take a haynet and feed if boxing; take a short feed if riding. Do not forget the grooming kit and hoof oil (a little round the eyes and nose of a dark-skinned pony will make him prettier). Leave your good clothes off until the last possible moment.

At the Show

When you arrive at the show, check in and get your number. Make sure you can hear the loudspeaker. If you have friends there, park or tie close to them, for your pony will feel more comfortable too. Detail somebody to be responsible for checking your number before you enter the ring, for you are likely to forget it yourself.

Warm up your pony but do not gallop ceaselessly up and down. If riding, show him the ring, the flags, the loudspeakers. If showing in hand, especially where presence and action are paramount, leave the pony in the trailer until the last possible moment, for he will show himself better.

If you have ridden to a show or rally, dismount as soon as you arrive. Unsaddle and give your short feed, making sure the pony has a rest before going in the ring.

In-hand classes
You will be expected to walk the pony away from the judge and trot back before standing square. The pony should look alert while he stands, not dreary (train him by crackling sweetpapers above and in front of his nose, so he reaches to your hand with interest, stretching his neck).

Riding classes
You will be expected to do a small show, which you should have practised until perfect: walk, trot, canter on both legs, and square standstill. Do not attempt too long or complicated a pattern. Do not allow your nerves to make you ride stiffly, for it will have the same effect on your pony. If she trots out well, overtake on the inside so you catch the judge's eye.

Leading-rein classes
Leading-rein classes are often a disappointment: the judge will generally pick an unsuitable, overbred, overfed and overlively creature rather than your excellent and trusted granny.

Jumping
Warm up a little before going over the practice jump. Make this low at first, then raise it. Do not allow other competitors to force you into doing high jumps before your pony is ready. Timing your warm-up is important and difficult. You will know best how excited your pony should be when he enters the ring. Do not stand in line waiting to enter the ring for he will get stiff and cold.

In any kind of a competition, however disappointed, do not criticize the judge or complain loudly. Everybody experienced knows that all judges are biased!

Gymkhana
A gymkhana consists of a number of races and games: bending in and out of a line of poles, sack race, apple bobbing, musical sacks, lead and ride, and so on. Most are divided into classes by age, and are arranged to be fun. Having a pony that leads well and will gallop from

Pony Club mounted games

and to a standstill easily, and being quick to get on and off, are important in a gymkhana. Practise against your friends or you will get left at the start at your first gymkhana. If the gymkhana is part of a larger show it will probably be held at the end, so do not gallop your pony up and down the sidelines all day or he will be worn out by the time you need him.

194

Rallies

Rallies come in various types, some competitive, some not. All of them usually involve a long day, so do not tire your pony unnecessarily and do not go unless she is fit. Do not sit on her for long periods; always dismount while waiting, for standing still with your weight on her tires her back. After a long day, ride home slowly, and remember that it is too much strain on tired legs that causes problems.

Endurance riding

Endurance riding, which is gaining popularity, is a form of rally or competition (some are races) that puts little nervous strain on the horse and does not need an expensive or highly bred animal. The only requirement is fitness, which you must gain through hours of training over months. Vet checks held at regular intervals along the route make sure you are not overstraining your pony. Most endurance rides require a speed of 8 mph cross-country, which can only be achieved with a variety of paces; try to develop an easy, ground-covering canter during training. Rules differ, so check before entering.

After a long day, coddle your pony. Bring him home slowly; water him, feed him well, twice if necessary; make sure he is warm and comfortable. If you suspect that the day has been hard on his legs, hose them and bandage them with cold water padding immediately you return. Next day check his legs carefully for signs of strain. If he is stabled, turn him out or take him for a walk, but do not leave him standing nor exercise him hard.

25 Difficult Behaviour

Left to themselves, ponies do not have problems. Their 'difficult' behaviour only happens when we try to force them into situations they fear or dislike and are then unable to cope with their objections. All experienced riders have at some time or another come up against horses they found difficult or even impossible, so if you have problems with your pony, do not despair or be too proud to admit it. Problems are a good opportunity to learn.

Ponies are naturally cooperative and friendly if they are treated properly, but your idea of what is proper may not be theirs. It even varies from pony to pony, so be prepared to change your handling if necessary. It is no use persisting with handling that produces bad behaviour in the belief that you are 'right' and the pony 'naughty'. What works between the two of you is more important than an artificial idea of 'correctness'. As you get to know more ponies you will find that many have strange quirks which their owners find quite acceptable.

Finding the cause of the bad behaviour points the way to its treatment. Generally beating the pony only makes matters worse. Ponies do not think of you as 'master' if you hurt them; they just dislike you and wish to leave.

Common causes of difficult behaviour are:

Bad riding or bad handling   Tension, wrong use of punishment, heavy hands, leaning forward, not using your legs and wrong use of the aids will all make even the best-mannered pony behave badly. Check this is not your problem by watching a more experienced person ride your pony; or ask a good riding school for an advice session.

Trauma   A pony never forgets a bad incident or accident and may take years to recover from the horror of it. He will behave nervously and sillily whenever reminded of it. For example, a head-shy pony may have been beaten over the head, or forcibly haltered when wild, many years ago; many ponies are nervous of gates after having been caught in one. Be slow and patient with such a pony; do not force him into the situation that frightens him in the hope of curing him, but teach him to trust you in other ways instead, until he trusts you in that one too.

Stabling and overfeeding   Being kept in, alone, and/or fed too much concentrated food are causes of a great deal of difficult behaviour: overexcitement in many forms, friskiness or nervousness, stable vices such as weaving, crib-biting and wind-sucking, biting and general irritability. There is no reason why even the most valuable of ponies should not have a companion and go out for several hours a day.

Discomfort   Too heavy a hand on too harsh a bit, too small a bit, an ill-fitting saddle or bridle, and pain, particularly in the back, can cause head-shaking, wriggling, turning to bite the rider, bucking, rearing and refusal: irritable or angry-seeming behaviour. Experiment with different tack; feel the back very carefully before and after exercise. Back problems are commoner than is usually thought, and can be helped by good massage. Tension and fear can cause back pain, which then provokes more tension and fear, and so on.
   Sharp teeth or wolf teeth are also a reason for dislike of the bit.

Habit   Bad habits can go on for years after the reason for them has disappeared. Like nail-biting or smoking in people, some horse habits are easily started but hard to stop. Head-shaking, for example, may start because a browband is too tight but may then persist throughout a lifetime of well-fitting bridles. In older ponies with strong, apparently causeless habits, the only 'cure' may be physically preventing the behaviour. However, this should always be the last resort because if there is a current reason for behaving badly, such as discomfort, the pony will find another, and perhaps worse, way of showing it.

Character Some ponies are more nervous and highly strung than others, and handling which works with one type does not necessarily work with another. Ponies are all individuals. Learn to adapt; take note of the signs of nervousness and tension that show the pony is unhappy. However, occasionally there is a genuine personality clash and both pony and owner would be better off with someone else; hence the importance of good, experienced advice when buying.

Age Young ponies may be nervous and excitable. They need patience and sympathy. They often get upset if you apply the aids in a different way from their first trainer. They need praise to show them what is expected, not force or punishment. Older ponies are calmer but they have also often learned how to avoid doing what they are asked, especially when ridden by young children. It is nonsense to tell a child to master a pony that is far stronger and wilier than himself; instead he must be helped to grow in confidence and competence. He should also be taught to be kind to his pony: most children are rough, demanding and ungrateful, which is what makes the ponies uncooperative in the first place.

Naughtiness Very rarely a cause of bad behaviour, except in the preceding case or when a lively pony's sense of jolly fun does not coincide with yours.

Season Some mares become silly when in season.

If you get a pony that you find difficult to manage at certain times, remember that her behaviour is bound to change within a few months simply as a result of having a new owner. In the meantime work on the areas in which you get on well together and avoid the difficulties, rather than getting involved in battles you may not win. Do not make these permanent no-go areas, but rather concentrate on building up a good, firm, trusting partnership, expanding this until you can gradually tackle the things you found impossible before. Most likely you will find that the difficulty has vanished, but if not you will at least have the advantage of knowing the pony thoroughly and having her trust you.

If you find that the pony is developing difficult behaviour, you are doing something she finds unacceptable. Change it.

Particular Problems

Hard to catch

Causes: because the pony has been chased and trapped in the past, and therefore gets into a running-away frame of mind; because he prefers his field to you.

Remedy: persist; never give up trying. Keep walking steadily to one side; do not run or herd him. Be confident: some people approach ponies with such an air of certainty that the ponies give in immediately, having led someone else a merry chase for hours. Always take a titbit or a bucket; always give another on releasing; always let his first and last impressions be pleasant. With a difficult youngster, catch her several times just to feed her. With a pony that becomes uncatchable on good summer grass, teach her to tether.

Bad about feet

Causes: fear, bad experience, habit.

Remedy: do not be put off by protest. Be satisfied with a little at first. Reward even the raising of a foot. If the pony lashes out in a frightening way, stand by her flank and stroke gently down her leg with a stick, so she kicks out without hurting you. She will finally get tired of kicking if you go on: pick up her foot briefly then. If you jump back in fear every time the pony makes a fuss about raising a foot you will make her worse.

Eats grass when ridden

This is especially common in children's ponies too strong for the child to hold.

Remedy: run a string from the front D of the saddle or the bar that holds the stirrup leather, through the bit and round to the other side. Tie it so that it is long enough for the pony to move his head freely while walking, but not long enough for him to reach the ground. You may then need a crupper to stop the saddle slipping forward.

Shying
Causes: nervousness, too tight a rein, overfreshness. Shying is really a way of looking at surprising objects, so the tighter the rein the more likely the pony is to jump sideways; on a looser rein he can move his head.

Remedy: keep a light rein, sit firmly and reassure the pony when approaching something he may shy at by rubbing his neck, letting him slow down and encouraging him to examine whatever is worry-ing him. If shying from freshness, reduce his oats or concentrates.

Napping (turning round fast to run home or backing up)
Causes: fear of what is in front, dislike of being in front or alone.

Remedy: keep your rein short but loose, so that the pony is not stopped from going forward freely, but can be stopped from turning round fast. Use your legs firmly. A kind, firm rider will cure a napper by offering sympathy and reassurance whenever the pony's nervous-ness increases, but a harsh rider will panic him more. With an older pony, if you suspect he is taking advantage of a weak rider, improve the rider's control by schooling or make sure the pony is ridden in company.

If the pony does turn round, keep turning her until she faces away from home again, and use your legs to urge her forwards.

Jibbing (stopping)
Causes: fear or dislike of going forwards; back pain.

Remedy: a lighter hand, a lighter bit, gaining the pony's confidence; good use of your leg to urge the pony forwards. If she runs back, pulling the reins will not stop her but will make her run back faster.

Rearing
Causes: fear, heavy hands, too harsh a bit, pain in the mouth or back. Rearing is an extreme case of not going forwards: it is as if the pony's fear makes a wall in front of him.

Remedy: at the time, lean well forward with your hands right forward (round his neck if necessary) so you do not pull him over backwards, and kick him forward. When the pony lands, make sure you put no pressure on the bit, and calm him.

In general, improve your hands; change the bit for a softer one; check his teeth and back. Keep the pony relaxed and moving forward well; ride with a companion.

Rearing is dangerous, especially for the novice, and it is counted as a vice. If you find you have bought a habitual rearer, return him. If the pony starts to rear after you have had him some time, your hands or bit are probably at fault.

Bucking

Causes: usually play; sometimes irritation or pain. Some ponies buck because the saddle is uncomfortable or your weight is back over a sore loin; most do it from high spirits; very few really mean to get rid of you, though a pony that does drop you will certainly enjoy scampering around for a while.

Remedy: at the time, lean backwards and kick the pony on hard while pulling his head up. He cannot buck and accelerate at the same time. Cut out oats and heating food; turn out or lunge a stabled pony before riding, encouraging him to get the bucks out of his system first; try trotting for a couple of miles to use up energy before cantering.

Running away

Causes: fun; bad riding; terror (bolting).

Remedy: lean back with your feet forward and brace yourself to pull. You cannot stop a runaway without using your weight, or with a steady pull. Give a little, while shortening your reins, then give a series of heaves to break the rhythm. You may have to pull the pony round in circles. When riding a pony likely to run away, relax and use a short but loose rein; pressure on the mouth or tension in your leg will help the pony collect himself ready for the off.

If the pony is fit, make him go on and on galloping after he has had enough until he is exhausted, then school him at a trot for as long as you can. This will make him think twice next time. Do not do this with an unfit, young or excitable pony.

Harsh hands and a hard bit can cause running away, so do not assume you need a stronger bit. Ask a more experienced person to ride the pony and advise you.

A jolly, well-fed pony likes a good gallop from time to time. However, too much galloping and racing, especially in the same place or when heading home, will encourage a pony to start taking off with you. If he does, change your ways before the habit gets unmanageable.

Very few ponies really bolt, that is, run away in terror; usually they startle, run a short way and then stop. Always allow such a pony to calm down and examine whatever frightened her, rather than punishing her. When a pony bolts unstoppably, remember that she cannot see well, so you may be safer baling out than heading for disaster.

Overexcitable pony

Causes: overfeeding and under-exercising; temperament; special fears; bad riding.

Remedy: always lean back, relax, keep your rein short but loose. Hanging on to a pony's mouth and leaning forward are bound to excite him. Be determined to keep to the pace you want; relax while you are doing that, but check him immediately he speeds up. Abusing the pony's mouth will make him fight.

Overconfinement, loneliness and overfeeding make ponies excitable. Reduce the concentrates, even if it means letting the pony down so his appearance suffers. Reduce his energy to a level where you can manage it; increase the work before the food. From here you have a basis on which to start building, which is impossible while you are battling.

Some ponies hot up in company, some alone, some going home, some behind others. Tackle the difficult areas gradually and sneakily rather than aiming to win in a straight fight.

Kicking

Causes: self-defence.

Remedy: many rather nervous horses will kick occasionally when you rush behind them or move in a startling way. Teach yourself not to. Some kick when you touch their hind legs or rump; with these you need to stand in a safe place and work steadily with the bad area, little by little (see chapter 15).

Serious, purposeful kickers will not be stopped by being punished, for they already feel they are being attacked. Avoid being kicked and work hard at gaining the pony's goodwill and keeping him in conditions that make him less miserable and irritable. However, a pony that has simply not learned manners can do so by being hit with a rope when he threatens to kick or just as he kicks.

Biting

Causes: attack, either playful or serious; irritation. A pony that bites a lot (there are few) is vicious. Usually this has come from badly timed punishment in early training, so the pony, often an affectionate one, feels attacked out of the blue.

Remedy: if you need to slap a pony for biting, do so very fast or not at all. Many ponies bite because they are strung up from being overfed, overconfined and under-exercised (especially stallions), and only changing the conditions will alter the behaviour. If the pony bites when being girthed up, take extra care when doing this and use a padded girth or girth cover for the pony is thin-skinned.

Stallion-like behaviour

Attacking other geldings, especially when mares are around, herding and mating with mares, roaring and screaming at other ponies, rearing, insisting on smelling other ponies' dung and dunging on it are behaviours that geldings do not normally show. They are, however, normal to a stallion. If your gelding behaves like this, to the point that you find him uncontrollable in company, you may have a rig or ridgeling. This is a male pony in which only one testis has descended, the other remaining in the body. If the descended testis has been cut, he will appear to be a gelding, though the remaining testis will produce hormones that tell him he is a stallion. It is sometimes possible to remove the remaining testis, but requires major surgery.

However, if your gelding produces some of these behaviours but is generally controllable, it is likely he has been gelded late, after he has grown up as a stallion and learned to behave as one. If you are in doubt, ask the vet to test for male hormones in his blood. Rigs are

Welsh mountain pony stallion crib-biting. In this pony the habit is so strong that he still crib-bites even when kept outside. As he sucks in air he makes a grunting noise and arches his neck so the underneath muscles stand out. The choice of a wooden surface at this height is typical.

This is a very well-bred pony, with a lovely head, good neck and well laid-back shoulder. However, keeping him inside during the breeding season in order to get him into show condition caused such stress that he started this incurable habit. He has changed the shape of his neck and simply cannot be got into good condition now, for he will not eat enough outside and cannot be kept in

204

confused, often dangerous animals and are not fit for children to ride. If you have been sold a rig as a gelding, return him.

Stable vices

Causes: constant stabling, overconfinement. There are a number of characteristic habits that constantly stabled ponies may develop. In weaving the pony stands by the door rocking from side to side; in crib-biting he takes the top of the door or manger in his teeth and gulps air; in wind-sucking he gulps air without holding anything. Walking the box, kicking the walls, pawing the door, head-tossing and snapping at passers-by are also common. These habits are almost unknown among ponies given enough freedom and are an expression of the terrible stress that stabled ponies feel.

Remedy: stable vices are generally incurable, though mechanical devices do sometimes prevent them (barred doors for weaving, removing all possible surfaces for crib-biting, a collar for wind-sucking). They are also copied by other ponies nearby. As the pony spends a good deal of time at his habit, he generally loses condition.

The only real cure, which must be put into operation as soon as the habit is noticed, is to relieve the pony's misery by keeping him out. If this is truly impossible, arrange a different type of stabling, for instance, a covered yard or open barn where he can live with companions and does not feel so confined.

26 Simple Health Problems and How to Deal with Them

Fortunately a native pony, regularly exercised and kept outdoors, will often live thirty-odd years without a day's sickness; more highly bred ponies are more delicate. Stabled ponies are more liable to sickness because of their unnatural lifestyle.

A healthy pony has bright eyes, a clean nose, a lively interest in what goes on and a supple skin. Make a habit of running your hand over your pony every day, for a sick pony's skin changes before other symptoms appear, becoming harsh to the touch. The coat becomes lifeless and staring; the legs may fill, that is, become puffy from standing motionless. Unless suffering from laminitis or colic, sick ponies rarely lie down or roll. Some diseases make the pony abnormally nervous, particularly in the stable. Ponies do not tolerate sickness or pain well; after all, in the wild they would be the first to be caught by wolves or lions, so they are frightened and usually seem as if they feel doomed. This means that careful nursing, kind attention and company means a great deal to them in sickness.

The First-Aid Kit

A simple, essential first-aid kit comprises bandages, gamgee or soft padding, antibiotic powder, mild disinfectant, fungicidal spray (sheep foot-rot spray), surgical spirit, fly repellent and Stockholm tar.

Nursing Notions

Stabling a sick pony

Warmth and good ventilation are essential, as is a nourishing, laxative diet. An outdoor pony suddenly brought in is prone to constipation and colic, swollen legs and lack of fresh air. He should be walked out twice daily, tempted with small, appetizing feeds and have his water changed frequently. Rug him up well and leave the stable doors and windows wide open.

Heat and cold

Cold takes down swelling immediately after an injury. Apply either iced water or cold water from a hosepipe for twenty minutes. Padding soaked in iced water can be applied under bandages. You can also make icepacks by putting mashed potato or stiff porridge in a plastic bag, moulding it over the affected part, cooling it in the 'fridge and then bandaging it in place.

Hot and cold water, applied alternately, stimulate the circulation, and therefore healing, when the danger of swelling is past.

Heat draws out pus. Apply hot salted water (hot fomentations), as hot as you can bear, several times daily, or use a poultice.

Poulticing

A kaolin poultice is made by heating an open tin of kaolin in boiling water, spreading an inch-thick layer on a piece of clean sheet, and applying this while hot. Cover the poultice with kitchen foil, which helps to keep the heat in, padding and a bandage. This takes some organization so make sure everything is ready before you apply the poultice. Leave on for twelve to twenty-four hours. Animalintex is a ready-prepared dressing that you heat before applying.

Bandaging

Stable bandages run from coronet to knee, exercise bandages from above the pastern only. When bandaging a hock or knee, take a rectangle of cloth and tear the two short sides into a series of little ribbons, leaving the centre square section whole. Place the central section over the joint and tie the ribbons in a series of bows. A bandage top and bottom help secure the dressing. When poulticing a foot, put the whole foot into a sturdy plastic bag, cover this with cloth (socks are best) and bandage well above the coronet to secure.

Injuries

Wounds Check any severe bleeding by pressing on the artery nearer to the heart than the cut. Very cold water or an icepack will also help to check bleeding. Wash out the wound with mild disinfectant (nothing stronger than you would use on yourself) and dress with antibiotic powder.

A badly injured pony will suffer from shock, so keep him warm.

It is important that deep wounds heal from the bottom upwards. Ponies' skin tends to heal over the top first, trapping a little pocket of infection underneath and letting it fester until the whole area bursts open in an abscess. Prevent this by washing the wound daily if necessary with mild salt solution; a lotion made of cranesbill (wild geranium) boiled in water promotes faster healing and will prevent infection. If cuts are accompanied by bruising, bathe with comfrey lotion or, for example with broken knees (see glossary), bandage on a paste of boiled comfrey leaves, which remove bruising and promote healing. Most cuts, except those on the cannon bone, where the skin will gape and scar, and those low on the leg, which may get infected by mud, are best left uncovered.

Severe cuts will need stitching. If you think this is necessary, apply cold compresses (pads soaked in ice water) and call the vet immediately, for once the wound swells it cannot be stitched.

Vets tend to want to inject penicillin after injury as a precaution. This is usually unnecessary unless infection has set in. Aim to prevent infection by care rather than by antibiotics, for these drugs upset a pony's digestion.

Sprains Apply cold immediately. Most likely to be sprained are the front tendons from hard work when unfit or tired, too much galloping over very soft going, and so on. The damage is usually not obvious until the next day, when the tendons at the back of the cannon bone are swollen and hot to touch. After cooling, apply support bandages, which should be firm over thick soft padding. If the padding is not thick enough the bandage will cut into the swelling flesh and cause more damage. Repeat the cooling three times a day for several days.

208

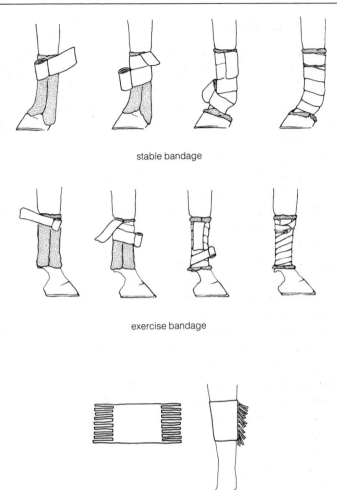

stable bandage

exercise bandage

many-tailed bandage

Figure 29 Bandages

Follow this with alternate heat (hot water) and cold and keep rebandaging. When the pony is sound, exercise with care in exercise bandages. After exercise cool the legs with surgical spirit and use support bandages.

209

Lameness

It is sometimes surprisingly difficult to decide which leg a pony is lame on, even when you can see he is going unevenly. Watch him trotting towards and away from you. If lame in the front foot, he dips his head as the good foot hits the ground; if in the rear, he drops his quarter on the lame side. Watch or ride him up- and downhill: if lame in front he will be worse going downhill, if behind, worse uphill.

The major causes of lameness are: an abscess in the foot, caused by a puncture wound; other injuries; bad shoeing or shoes being left on too long; concussion, especially in young ponies, whose legs will not stand up to much trotting on the road; strain due to too much work, especially galloping or jumping, when unfit; strain or injury due to bad conformation; laminitis.

Constantly compare the lame leg with its sound partner, feeling for heat, swelling and other differences. If no obvious bruise, injury or tendon strain shows up, examine the foot. It is said that 90 per cent of lameness in front is below the knee.

Feel for heat or other signs of inflammation (enlarged blood vessels on the outer side of the pastern just above the foot, unusual flinching when you tap the sole of the foot). If there is heat in both feet, suspect laminitis; if in one, suspect an abscess under the sole caused by a puncture wound. Either case needs a vet. If there is tenderness without heat, suspect bruising from slamming the foot down on a sharp stone or from corns caused by shoes being left on too long.

In an unshod pony bruising and gravel often cause tenderness. Gravel gets into the white line, the soft layer where the outer wall of the hoof meets the sole. It works its way up, finally emerging as an abscess (quittor) on the coronet, unless speedily dug out. Pack the hole with shredded hempen bale string soaked in Stockholm tar or the problem will recur. If the pony is newly shod, the blacksmith may have pinched him, that is, pricked the quick with a nail: he should be called back immediately.

Always clean out the grooves of the frog thoroughly. Thrush is a smelly infection here and on the sole; it is caused by damp ground. Spray with foot-rot spray daily and move the pony to dry ground. Wet conditions can also make heels soft and sore; paint them with Stockholm tar and move the pony.

The front heels may also be bruised and cut from overreaching, that is, the front of the back foot hitting the back of the front foot. This can be due simply to the way the pony moves or to the shoes being left on too long. Tell the blacksmith what has happened and equip yourself with overreach boots. Bad movement also causes brushing, when the inside of one foot hits the coronet or pastern of the opposite foot. For this you need brushing boots and a blacksmith skilled in remedial work.

Examine the coronet for bruising, puncture wounds or signs of quittor as well as brushing. The coronet is highly sensitive and injury here is painful. Poultice if you suspect inflammation: poulticing and hot salt water will not harm healthy tissue and sometimes produce surprising results.

The fetlock joint may be bruised and inflamed. Check carefully that it matches its partner. Ringbone and sidebone are incurable bony growths on the fetlock and pastern and give intermittent trouble, especially if the legs have been banged by trotting on the road. Concussion is also the cause of splints (see chapter 2), which are bony lumps a little way down the inside of the cannon bone. These almost always arise in ponies under the age of five. When a splint is setting it is painful, hot and inflamed; rest and liniment may take it down. After a splint has set it usually gives no trouble, although technically it is an unsoundness and a pony with a splint will get nowhere in a show ring.

A swollen leg (big leg) may be due to tendon strain or filling (stocking up) in a stabled pony. It can also be due to an infection somewhere below the swelling, usually in the foot.

Knees seldom give trouble unless they have been hit; old ponies sometimes get arthritis in the knee.

If you suspect a shoulder strain, pull each front leg forward in turn. The pony will be reluctant to allow her leg to be pulled if she has a bad shoulder. Turn her in a circle: a shoulder injury makes her lamer when the bad shoulder is outside. Shoulder strain rarely occurs except after an accident or fall, but it is often suspected simply because no other cause of lameness can be found.

If none of the above fits the case, look to the foot again. Also examine the leg minutely for a thorn, especially if you have been in rough country. Blackthorn, which is easily driven through the skin, is painful and difficult to find.

In the hind leg most lameness is caused by hock problems, which produce different types of swelling: bone spavin, bog spavin or thoroughpin, according to whether the inflammation affects bone or tendon. Bone spavin, like ringbone, is really arthritis. Hock lameness needs a vet.

Old ponies get rheumatism, which used to be known as flying lameness from its habit of varying dramatically. A New Zealand rug with an underblanket provides great relief to rheumatic hips.

Other Problems

Abscess Puncture wounds, blackthorn or other stabbing injuries can cause an abscess, a hard, hot, painful lump which has to burst to release the trapped pus. Either poultice or apply hot salt water, as hot as you can bear, three or four times daily for half an hour at a time. This will bring it to a head and encourage it to burst. Clean it out daily with heat followed by hydrogen peroxide and keep it open so it heals from below.

Azoturia (setfast) Azoturia is seen in fit, hard-working, stabled ponies after a day off when the feed has not been cut down. The pony is obviously stiff and in pain, and the urine is dark. Call the vet. On the next rest day, give vegetables instead of concentrates.

Bots The larvae of gadflies which lay their eggs on ponies' hair. If the eggs are eaten, through the pony scratching his leg with his mouth, the larvae hatch and develop in the stomach. They are passed out as pupae in the dung, but meanwhile make the pony lose condition worse than worms. Most wormers do not get rid of bots, so if you have repeatedly wormed your pony without good results, and if you have seen the small yellowish eggs on his legs and shoulder, suspect bots and reworm with ivermectin.

Prevent bot infection by combing the eggs out with a fine-toothed comb; by providing a field shelter (ponies use shelters more in the summer than in the winter); or, if there are a lot of gadflies about, by rubbing old sump oil over the pony's upper legs and shoulders.

Bruises If noticed immediately, apply cold and tincture of arnica (which works wonders if you get bruised too). Bandaging a limb will help prevent a lump forming. However, the first sign of bruising often is a lump. Hot and cold fomentations will increase circulation and help disperse the bruise, and arnica will still be effective.

Choking   A greedy pony may choke on dry nuts or sugarbeet. Massage the lump formed and call the vet.

Colds   Ponies suffer from colds like us in the winter, especially in prolonged wet periods. Make sure they have enough shelter, warmth (rugs, warm food) and good bulk. If stabled, make sure there is plenty of air or the pony will start coughing too. Inhalations of Friar's Balsam give great relief to snotty noses: put a handful of hay in a duffel bag or plastic carrier bag, pour in half a pint of boiling water, add the balsam as directed, and pull the bag up over the pony's nose, fastening it over his head with laces. Allow him to breathe the fumes for 10–15 minutes several times daily. If you cannot get Friar's Balsam, a few drops each of menthol and eucalyptus will do. Garlic oil in the food helps too.

Cold back   Some ponies dip their backs when first the saddle is put on or you get on. This can be due to back pain but may also be because the pony objects to the saddle being pressed down on a cold, wet back. Ask someone experienced to check the pony's back. If there seems to be no trouble, always dry the back thoroughly before saddling. Use a warm numnah or blanket, and put this and the saddle on for several minutes before doing up the girth tightly.

Colic   Horses do not vomit or belch, so if something upsets the digestion it causes great pain. There are different types of colic. Sharp pains are caused by worms moving through the gut wall, by drinking icy water when hot, or bad food. Changes in food, especially if an outdoor pony is suddenly stabled and fed dry food, cause blockages. Colic almost always occurs in stabled ponies and stress may be an important factor, rather like ulcers in people.

A colicky pony is restless, stamping, lashing his tail, looking in a puzzled way at his side, and rolling in a frantic and violent way as if tortured by ants. He may sweat in patches; his breathing rate increases. If his belly is totally silent for minutes on end when you press your ear to it, he probably has a blockage. This type of colic is not so painful. The main danger in acute colic is that in rolling violently the pony will twist his gut, which is usually fatal.

Call the vet, but meanwhile keep the pony warm and walk him gently to prevent him rolling. In a mild case of blockage, drench with a pint of liquid paraffin (mineral oil). Add a tablespoonful of sugar to the oil and put it in a plastic bottle: a flat-sided one is best. Throw the pony's lead rope over a high branch or beam so you can pull his head up, put the bottle in the side of his mouth and squeeze gently. Take care only to give a little at a time, massaging the pony's throat so he swallows, or he may get it in his lungs. Let his head down from time to time. Drenching is a messy affair.

Any case of colic must be followed by a laxative diet: sugar beet, carrots (lots) and linseed.

Cough Many stabled ponies give a cough on first galloping. However, if a pony coughs more than that, find out why. Infectious coughs usually come with a snotty nose and evident sickness. Non-infectious coughs are caused by musty hay, poor ventilation or allergies (heaves). Lungworm, caught from donkeys, also causes coughing.

Newmarket cough (known as *the* cough) is a particularly infectious and serious form; other coughs, various viruses, are milder. If there is an infection the glands under the chin are swollen.

A pony with a cough should not be worked. On the whole she is better outside, warmly rugged, and well fed with laxative foods. If she sickens, or if you have heard that there is an infectious cough in the area, isolate her and call the vet. The pony may have to be stabled and nursed well, for some infectious coughs are serious and can prove fatal if neglected. Care must be taken that bedding is dust-free, that the hay is soaked before feeding and that the pony gets plenty of fresh air.

Diarrhoea Usually caused by sudden change to rich food, like spring grass. Keep the pony on hay for several days. Make sure he is drinking well. Make the change to rich food more gradual. If this is not the cause and the pony seems ill, call the vet as it may be caused by an infection.

Filled leg Swollen legs, usually from the hock down, are most often seen in a stabled pony left unexercised. It is uncomfortable for the pony but disappears if you exercise him.

Flu Horse flu is extremely contagious, that is, it is spread by droplets breathed out by an infected pony, so it can be carried on clothes, etc. Keep your pony away from other horses if you hear of it in the district. It is now possible to inoculate against horse flu. A pony with flu is obviously sick, with a high temperature (feel the ears), lack of appetite, depression, weepy eyes, runny nose and sometimes swollen legs. Keep him warm, call the vet, and nurse him well.

Galls Sore places caused by ill-fitting or dirty saddles and girths.

214

he first sign is extreme irritation when the area is stroked; on careful xamination a hot spot may be found. If the skin is not broken or hafed, surgical spirit may be applied. If there is an open sore, a dilute olution of alum will harden the new skin. Galls are like bedsores and espond to bedsore cures.

If the withers are galled by the saddle, take heed at the first sign of rritation. Wither galls can turn into abscesses, causing a fistula or ocket of pus down the shoulder. This is extremely difficult to clear as he pus has to drain upwards. Galls also develop under the seat of a adly stuffed saddle. The pony cannot be used until the sore has leared, and the same saddle cannot be used again. White hair isually grows on areas that have been galled.

Girth galls develop behind the elbow where the skin is thin and are aused by dirty girths. They can be guarded against in a thin-skinned ony by using a padded girth or fur girth cover. An open gall should e dressed and covered with a big pad of cottonwool and a sponge inder the girth. If properly protected, galls heal better if the pony is till used. An area once galled is likely to gall again, so use a soft girth.

Heaves (COPD: chronic obstructive pulmonary disease)   An illergy to mould and fungus spores in hay and straw; sometimes to ollen. In other words, it is like hay fever in people though the effects re more like asthma. The pony is short of breath, wheezy and oughs. Most often seen in stabled ponies, heaves develops gradally and is incurable although it can be controlled. The pony must be ept away from hay and straw. If possible she should be turned out; if lot, she should be bedded on peat or paper and fed on grass pellets, ugarbeet and the like. Heaves causes changes in the lungs that finally esult in what used to be called broken wind. If you suspect it, call the et for a proper diagnosis so that you can guard against it before too nuch damage is done.

Laminitis   Laminitis is common in small fat native ponies kept on good grazing, especially in spring, though any pony can get it after aiding the feed bin. It is an inflammation of the layer of the hoof that orresponds to our nailbed and is caused by too much carbohydrate n the blood. It usually occurs in the front feet only and is extremely ainful. The pony stands on the backs of his heels and refuses to nove, especially on hard ground. He may even lie down with his feet out in front of him, as if about to get up. The feet are hot and the blood essel in the pastern is enlarged.

215

Call the vet immediately. Laminitis makes the hoof change shape and it can collapse entirely so that the pedal bone drops right through the sole, so prompt attention is needed. Make the pony move on soft ground for, say, a couple of minutes every half hour. This will help the circulation in the feet but you will feel cruel.

Reduce the pony's weight immediately by keeping him in and feeding only a little hay and turnips; or tether him on poor grazing.

After a pony has had laminitis his sole drops, so he is more likely to bruise it; his heel becomes weak; horizontal ridges grow round the hoof, which grows long and flat. Even with great care these changes will last a year or two. The pony is also more likely to get laminitis again, which means that you must keep him thin and on poor grazing in spring. Have the blacksmith every month; even if the shoes are not worn he will reset them so the new hoof grows properly.

Lice   A pony with lice scratches, especially his chest, neck and rump. He may even rub his chest bald or tear it on barbed wire. Lice are common on shaggy ponies in winter. They are very small and pale brown, so they are difficult to see. Check by lifting the forelock and looking at its roots. You may find nits (eggs), yellowish specks on the hairs, there. Treat with louse powder, paying particular attention to the mane, neck, withers, shoulder and rump. Repowder every two weeks; the powder does not get rid of eggs, which take two weeks to hatch.

Mud fever   Large weepy scabs on the legs and heels caused by an organism in mud. They are painful and may cause lameness and swelling. Keep the pony out of mud; treat with a soothing greasy cream (e.g. zinc and castor oil cream). If the pony is stabled, wash the legs thoroughly after each ride and dry them carefully. Fine-skinned chestnut ponies with white legs are most prone.

Navicular disease   Navicular syndrome is a poorly understood condition that rarely affects ponies, though ones with Thoroughbred blood may be prone to it. As a result of changes in the navicular bone in the foot, the pony has a pottery, short-strided gait and points a forefoot when resting. The condition used to be thought incurable though cases caught early can now be treated. If your pony shows these symptoms with no obvious cause, call the vet for a proper diagnosis.

Rain scald (mud rash, weatherbeat)   Scabs on the back, loins and rump caused by an organism that thrives when the weather is wet

216

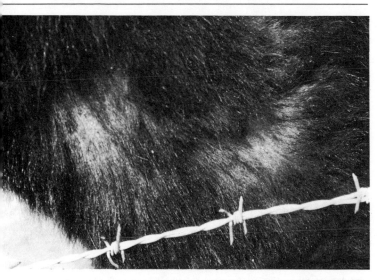

Lice. This pony has rubbed the under side of his neck bare in a typical way. In the middle of the right-hand bare patch you can see two lice

Severe rain-scald. In ponies kept out and ungroomed during a wet winter the hair first becomes clumped, as seen high on the hindquarter; scabs then form at the bottom of the clumps, which lift off leaving bare, weeping patches

217

for weeks on end. The waterlogged hair separates into sections, which lift off in a weepy scab. In a bad case the pony ends up bald. The only cure is to make sure the pony's back is dried and brushed every day, so good management will guard against it. Do not pick off the scabs, but rub almond or olive oil over them.

Ringworm Bald, sore, flaky patches on the face, neck and shoulder, often seen on cattle. Ringworm (which does not form rings) is a fungus that can be caught from infected posts, pens, girths, etc. Treat with fungicidal cream; disinfect all tack thoroughly.

Strangles An infectious disease affecting the throat. The pony has a stiff neck, snotty nose, lack of appetite and is evidently sick. The glands under the chin swell greatly so the pony has difficulty in swallowing and breathing. Eventually they burst open, discharging pus.

These glands also swell slightly whenever the pony has an infection, so swollen glands do not necessarily mean he has strangles. The vet will know if there is strangles in the area. However, a snotty nose, sickness, and swollen glands mean the pony has some sort of infection and needs the vet and careful nursing.

Sweet itch An allergy to midge bites which makes the pony scratch her mane and tail furiously in summer. The skin becomes thick and bald, the mane and tail short and tufty. The pony may become so sore as to be unridable. There is no certain cure except keeping the pony away from midges by stabling her in the summer or by covering her in an insect repellent that wards off midges. Some ponies are helped by large doses of garlic oil in the feed.

Tetanus (lockjaw) Paralysis and death caused by an organism commonly present in stables, yards, etc., and introduced into the body by a puncture wound, for instance, a nail penetrating the sole. After such a wound you should have the vet inoculate against tetanus immediately if it has not been done already.

Warts Warts are fairly common in young ponies, who grow out of them without any special treatment.

27 Make Do and Mend

Keeping a pony can be an expensive business: there is no end of fancy equipment and clothing to be had. However, if you are on a limited budget your money is best spent on feeding your pony properly, economizing on your tack, and caring well for what you have.

Apart from a bit and a saddle, a good deal of everyday gear can be made. Cut your bale string by the knots and save it carefully. The hemp sort does eventually rot, but ropes made of a mixture of plastic and hemp string are soft, strong, long-lasting and do not cause rope-burn. Ships' chandlers are a good source of rings and clips.

Lead ropes   A lead rope should be about 10 feet long. Plait six strands together and finish with a large knot.

Halter   Plait six or nine strands together until the rope is about 15 feet long. Tie one end into a loop with an overhand knot, so the loop is large enough to fit the pony's nose. Pass the rope over his head behind his ears and thread it through the noseband opposite your first knot, tying it so it does not slip. You will find the knots tighten after a while but as long as the halter fits snugly it will not come off.

Lunge line   This should be about 30 feet long. Six strands plaited together will be thick enough.

Tether rope   Once your pony is used to being tethered on a chain he should be safe on a rope. Homemade ropes are actually better than manufactured ones, as they do not burn and the pony can see them well. Make a thick rope about 30 feet long from a mixture of hemp twine and the brightest assortment of plastic twine you can find.

Bridle   The simplest bridle to make is the Western one-ear type. Plait six strands for the bridle and divide the plait round one ear. Despite the lack of a throatlatch, it should not come off unless your pony pulls back strongly when led. You will find neatly plaited reins comfortable to handle and non-slip in wet weather.

Haynet Using a haynet saves hay from being trampled in mud. Tie about twenty-four strings together in pairs and lay each pair over a removable bar. Tie each string to its neighbour, starting with the 2nd and 3rd strings, the 4th and 5th, the 6th and 7th and so on, using overhand knots about 4 inches below the bar. Now make another row of knots about 4 inches below the first, tying the 1st and 2nd, 3rd and 4th, 5th and 6th strings, etc. Continue making rows of knots, starting the next row with the 2nd string and the following one with the 1st again, until your have a square net. Slip it off the bar, double it over and tie up the sides to make a bag. Thread a different-coloured string through the top loops to hang it up with.

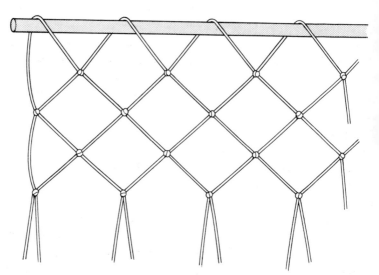

Figure 30 Making a haynet

Tape Soft nylon tape can be used to make gaily coloured, inexpensive tack for everyday use. The easiest way to fasten it is by burning holes through it with a hot skewer and tying it with shoelaces; you can also use rivets. A homemade bridle does not, of course, have to be adjustable.

Do not use nylon tape as a lunge line or you will burn your hands.

220

Breast harness   Use a surcingle with a padded girth as the breast-band. You will need a piece of string over the pony's neck to keep it up. The surcingle must be padded on either side of the pony's spine. Check carefully to see that the breastband is in the right place when the pony is pulling: if it is too high he will have difficulty breathing.

Seat belts padded with old clothes can be used for all sorts of homemade harness.

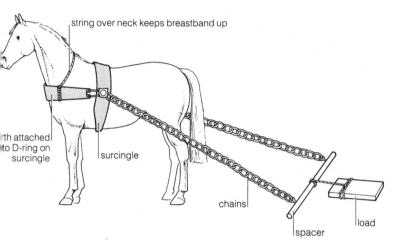

Figure 31 Simple breast harness

Pack saddle   For carrying loads slowly over even ground a pad from a heavy farm-cart harness can be used. This has a metal groove in which a chain normally runs. Loads of equal weight can be tied together and slung over it.

For more adventurous packing you need a proper pack saddle. Western or Spanish pack saddles are good if you can get one. A cavalryman's saddle (not the officer type) can also provide a good framework to adapt. However, you may be reduced to making one.

The safest sort to make is the sawbuck. Basically this is like a small sawhorse resting on two long floats that go each side of the pony's spine. Make your floats from two thick boards about 6 inches wide and 2 feet long, shaped and tapered to fit the pony. A good fit is important. Pad the underside of each float with sheepskin or cloth

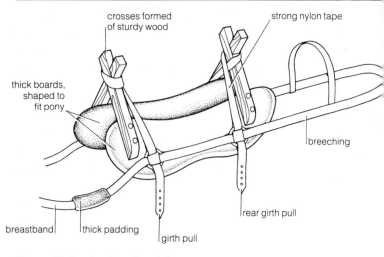

Figure 32 Sawbuck pack saddle

stretched tightly over shredded jerseys or horsehair. Make the crosses sturdy and bolt them on well.

You will need two girths, one at each end of the saddle. Tape slung round the crosses can hold a sturdy ring to hold the girth pulls. The rear girth prevents the saddle from tipping forwards but is never done up tightly. For rough work you will also need a breastband and breeching. These are best made from padded seat belts. Make sure the furnishings do not rub.

Always use a good thick blanket under a pack saddle. You can make panniers but frameless rucksacks serve perfectly well. Make sure they are evenly balanced (a small spring balance is useful) and hang the shoulder straps from the crosses. Lash the whole lot firmly so it does not flop when the pony goes fast. If you put a pack on top as well make sure it does not touch the pony's spine.

Care of leather tack   Keep your tack well oiled. If you often ride in the rain, make a waterproof saddle cover. Cut an old anorak, mackintosh or other waterproof fabric so that it fits over the whole saddle with an overlap of 4 inches all round. Fold over the outside half-inch round the edge, stitch and thread with elastic so the cover stays snug when fitted.

Mending tack   Clean out torn stitching and restitch through the same holes, using a blunt leather needle and linen thread. Saddlemakers use two needles, stitching through the same hole from both sides at the same time, but this is hard. You can produce the same effect by stitching in one direction, turning and stitching back again so that one continuous line of stitching is seen. You may need a pair of pliers to pull the needle through.

To make new stitching you need an awl, finely sharpened to a flat edge. Put the leather on a soft board and punch a row of holes, eight to an inch, as evenly as you can. If they are irregular you will have trouble matching them up. Trim the ends of the leather so as to form a smooth overlap before putting the two surfaces together and stitching.

You can also make effective, though ugly, repairs by punching small holes with a leather punch and riveting or tying the two pieces together.

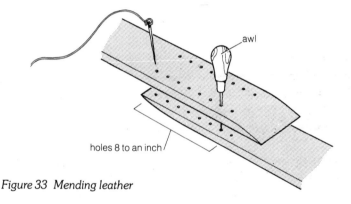

Figure 33 Mending leather

28 The End

Sadly, people outgrow and outlive ponies. However, it is part of your responsibility as a horseperson, having enjoyed what your pony had to give, to see that whatever end he comes to is a decent one.

Selling an outgrown pony can be hard. If you can do so through personal contact, so much the better. As with buying, farriers and the Pony Club are generally reliable in finding good homes. Do not sell your pony too cheap: anyone who cannot find the asking price may not be able to afford to feed him either. Try, as discreetly as possible, to find out what the prospective buyers are like and where they intend to keep him. Do not lie about his abilities or he will not find the right home.

Do not take the pony to a sale. You have no idea where he may end up: on a hook, bought by idiots, starved or worked to exhaustion, maybe. You may not know of the horrors that some ponies undergo but any RSPCA inspector will enlighten you.

Check up on your pony in his new home. Anyone sympathetic will understand that you would like to see him again. The new owner may need help; so may the pony. It is often difficult to be diplomatic if you are unhappy about his treatment, but people will reject advice if it is given rudely. A recommendation or even a present of a book you have found helpful may be a polite way of making your point.

A small old pony presents particular problems. Often the best move is to lend her rather than sell her for the few pounds she is worth, for then you can be sure she will not come to a sticky end. The Riding for the Disabled Association sometimes accepts old ponies, and their standards of care and handling are impeccable.

When a pony reaches the end of her days, do not wait until she is in misery before you put her down. Winters are hard on the old: consider the quality of her life rather than your sentiments. It is a consolation to know that in the end you have spared pain and suffering.

Ponies can be destroyed by shooting or injection. Shooting (with a captive bolt pistol, a humane destroyer) is harder on your nerves but is absolutely instantaneous if done by a skilled person. On the whole knackers are more practised at this than vets. The knacker will come with a van, hide it discreetly round the corner if you prefer, ask you to hold the pony with his head in a bucket of food and fit the humane destroyer quietly on his head. There is no fuss and death is instantaneous. The knacker will then take the body away and send you a tiny and heartrending cheque.

Death by injection, as is usual for dogs and cats, sounds better but probably isn't for the pony. Old dogs and cats are used to going to sleep in your arms; ponies hate to fall to the ground, and although it is said that they are no longer conscious, they do rather look as if their last minutes are spent in a fruitless and panic-stricken struggle to get up again.

Ponies only fetch the meat price if they are taken to a slaughter-house alive – hardly a fit end for a friend.

If you intend to bury your friend at home, you will need a very large hole.

Glossary of Horseman's Words and Terms

Only terms not explained in the text are defined here; for others, see the index.

back at the knee   Conformation defect: knee badly made so that the lower part of the leg slopes forwards.

bay   Rich reddish-brown colour with black mane and tail and black 'points' (lower parts of legs). Bright bay is the colour of a conker, dark bay almost black. Bay is a dominant colour, that is, in breeding it is a strong colour and can mask other colours genetically present.

black   There are two types of black. The more usual dilute black fades as the coat grows older so that each new coat shows pitch black against the browner old coat. This black is recessive. Pure black does not fade, is a fairly dominant colour, and is much rarer.

blaze   White stripe down the front of the face, from the forehead to the nose.

blister   Irritant paste or liniment applied to an old, cold injury or bony lump to increase the circulation and dissolve the lump.

blood   A 'blood' horse or pony is part or wholly Thoroughbred.

bolting   Running away in a blind panic. Most ponies accused of bolting are running away for fun, not from terror.

boring   Leaning down and forwards on the bit so as to avoid being controlled.

box foot   Upright, high-heeled foot. This type of foot is prone to navicular disease.

breeching   Part of harness that goes round a pony's rump, to stop a trap or cart.

226

bridoon   The snaffle bit of a double bridle.

broken knee   Knee scarred due to falling on road. An injury severe enough to make a scar will also damage the joint.

broken wind   'Heaves', see page 215. The pony coughs, wheezes and shows a double lift of the belly when breathing out after exercise.

brown   Chocolate brown with same-coloured mane and tail. The colour lacks the reddish or yellowish tinge seen in bays.

brushing   Knocking the inside of one foot against the opposite fetlock while moving.

calf knee   Back at the knee (q.v.).

cantle   Rear end of the saddle.

cavesson   Noseband strengthened with metal, for lunging, when the lunge line is attached to a ring on the front for greater control. A cavesson noseband is an ordinary noseband.

change of leg   Changing the leading leg when cantering, for instance at the crossover in a figure of eight. Normally done by dropping to a trot for a pace or two and setting off again on the other leg.

chestnut   i. Bright gingery-red colour, with similar mane and tail. Genetically rather a recessive colour.

   ii. Horny growth on the insides of the legs, above the knee and below the hock.

clicking   Sound made by one foot, usually the hind, hitting the other. Severe damage to the coronet can result unless remedial shoes or boots are used.

close-coupled   Short and powerful in the loin, a most desirable characteristic when great manoeuvrability is wanted, as in polo.

cold-blooded   Type originating from northern breeds, characterized by calm temperament, heavy bone, abundant winter coat, mane and tail, and hardiness.

colt   Uncastrated male horse or pony under three years old.

contact   Feel of the pony's mouth through the rein.

cowhocked   With weak hocks set so that the lower part of the leg turns out.

cream   Cream-coloured all over, with similar mane and tail. A blue-eyed cream has pink skin, a dark-eyed one dark skin.

crest   Top of the neck when well-developed into a curve, as seen in stallions.

cribbing   Crib-biting: sucking in air while holding the top of the door or manger etc. in the teeth.

diagonal   The two legs that move forwards simultaneously at the trot. The left diagonal is the left (near) fore and the right (off) hind. When schooling it is usual to trot on the outside diagonal, i.e. the seat comes down when the outside diagonal comes to the ground, changing the diagonal by sitting down for one pace when changing direction.

dish-faced   With a concave profile, as in Arabs.

dishing   Swinging the foreleg outwards when lifting it: generally more exaggerated at the trot. A fault in movement.

disunited   Cantering on one lead in front and the other behind, giving an extremely awkward, lumpy feel. A sign of great stiffness or possibly back pain.

dock   The part of the spine that runs down the tail. 'Docking' (now illegal) means cutting through this near to the body to bob the tail.

dressage   Advanced formal training which makes the horse light, supple and responsive.

dun   Cream, gold or brown with darker mane and tail, dorsal stripe and lower legs. A primitive, northern colour: most duns are very hardy. The rare blue dun is silver-grey (not roan) with darker points and stripe.

eventing   Competition with 3 phases: dressage, cross-country and show jumping, completed over one or three days.

ewe-necked   With a badly shaped neck, concave at the top and convex at the bottom.

feather   Long silky hair on the back of the fetlocks or, in heavy horses, on the lower legs in general.

filly   Female horse or pony under three years old.

firing   Inserting hot needles into sprained tendon or ligament to increase the circulation and promote healing. A horse that has been fired has a pattern of lines or dots on the cannon bones. Less often done nowadays as there is little proof that it works.

flying change   Change of leg at the canter without dropping to a trot.

forging   Hitting the underside of the front foot with the toe of the back foot. Careful shoeing can remedy this.

forward seat   Seat developed by Caprilli in the 1930s for fast cross-country or show jumping.

frog   V-shaped pad of gristle on the underside of the foot.

gelding   Castrated male horse or pony of any age.

goose-rumped   With a prominent point of croup but drooping rump and low tail-set: a weak conformation.

grey   With a mixture of dark and white hairs. There are various sorts of grey: iron grey, dapple grey; blues as in blue dun and blue roan; and white, which is called grey unless the pony is albino (with pink skin and eyes). Grey is a dominant colour. Most greys go whiter with age.

half-bred   Half Thoroughbred.

half-crown pieces   Dapples in the sheen on a pony's coat, usually seen in bays, blacks and chestnuts. A sign of prime condition.

halter   Rope head-harness for leading and tying.

hand   Four inches. The height of a pony is measured at the withers. Without a proper measuring stick the easiest way to measure height is by putting a spirit level on the pony's withers and recording the height on a pole.

hard mouth   Insensitive mouth. Generally due to years of abuse, as in riding school ponies.

headcollar   Leather or webbing harness.

headstall   Leather bridle from which the bit can be removed to make a headcollar. (US: Leather part of bridle.)

herd-bound   Pony that refuses to leave others.

herring-gutted   With a long, thin, narrow belly that is due to conformation rather than underfeeding.

hidebound   With tight, staring, lifeless skin: a sign of poor condition, dehydration, or sickness.

hogging   Shaving off the mane.

horse   Generally over 14.2hh, though more properly an entire i.e. uncastrated animal over 14.2.

hot-blooded   Type originating from southern or desert regions, excitable, fine-skinned, delicate, with fine, hard bone and feet.

impulsion   Pent-up forward-going energy.

in hand   Led rather than ridden or free.

jack   Male donkey.

jenny   Female donkey.

jibbing   Refusing to go forwards.

jute rug   Rug made of material like sacking, for wear in the stable.

laminae   Layers of tissue that form the horn of the hoof.

light in hand   Responsive to the rein and with the balance going up rather than down in front (c.f. on the forehand).

liver chestnut   Very dark chestnut, the colour of ox liver. May have same-coloured or flaxen (blond) mane and tail.

long reining   Driving a horse from the ground with two long reins, either from the side or from behind. An essential part of breaking to drive; may also be done when breaking to ride. Also called ground-driving in US.

lop-eared   Lacking the muscles necessary to prick the ears, which are therefore carried sideways and swung to and fro. Commoner in hunter types.

lunge   To drive the pony round in circles, usually on a single rein attached to the front of a cavesson.

mare   Female horse or pony over the age of three. A barren mare is one that is not in foal; a brood mare is one that is used for breeding only.

napping   Refusing to go by plunging, turning round etc.

near side   The horse's left side.

New Zealand rug   Waterproof canvas rug designed for continuous outdoor wear.

off side   The horse's right side.

on the bit   Pony which goes freely forwards while accepting a contact through the rein, neither raising his head above it (above the bit) nor ducking behind it (behind the bit).

on the forehand   Pony whose balance is tilted towards the front so that more weight is carried by the front legs. Such a pony is heavy in hand and slow to turn.

overreach   Cut or blow to the heel of the forefoot made by the toe of the hindfoot, caused by overlong foot, bad conformation or immaturity.

palomino   Bright chestnut or gold colour with white mane and tail; in US recognized as a breed. A heterozygous colour best obtained by crossing a chestnut with a blue-eyed cream, good palomino does not breed true although washier or flaxen-tailed versions may do.

piebald   Black and white, in large patches.

pigeon toed   With the toes pointing in: a conformation fault although a very mild case makes a pony quick off the mark.

plaiting   Moving the feet inwards at each step so they are placed one behind each other on the midline instead of each side of it. A bad defect in movement: a pony that plaits badly behind develops no power and may trip himself up. All donkeys plait.

pommel   Rise at the front of the saddle.

pony   Adult horse under 14.2hh. Polo ponies are also called ponies although the height restriction has been removed.

potbellied   With a blown-out belly, often a sign of worms.

pottery   Shuffling, as if lame all round.

poverty line   Vertical crease in the hindquarters running down each side of the tail. Seen especially in emaciated ponies: do not, however, confuse with the line shown by extremely fit, lean horses.

pulse   Normally 36–40 at rest. You can feel the pulse on the inner edge of the lower jawbone, with practice.

rig   Cryptorchid: male with one undescended testis.

roachbacked   With a straight or even convex back instead of the normal slight dip. A conformation fault.

roan   With a coat of white and other coloured hairs evenly mixed over most of the body surface, but less or no white on the legs and head. A strawberry roan has chestnut as the ground colour so that it appears pink with a chestnut head and legs; a blue roan is blue with grey or black legs; a bay roan is pink or grey with black legs and a brown head. Roaning increases with age.

roaring   Loud noise made while galloping by a horse with collapsed vocal cords: defect in wind. The noise can be cured by an operation called hobdaying.

Roman-nosed   With a convex nose, usually a sign of cold blood.

run up   With the belly fallen in: a sign that the horse has recently suffered strain from hard work, lack of food or water, or nervous stress (e.g. after a journey) and needs rest and food to replace weight loss.

sandcrack   Vertical crack running up the hoof. A bad sandcrack will not heal on its own but needs riveting together by the farrier.

seedy toe   Foul-smelling rot of the toe, running up the white line. Often follows laminitis if the pony is kept on wet ground.

sickle-hocked   With overbent hocks so that the cannon bone runs forwards, not vertically. A conformation defect.

skewbald   Brown and white, in patches.

snip   White mark on the lower end of the nose only.

sock   White pastern and fetlock, like an ankle-sock.

231

sorrel   Chestnut with a small amount of roan; in US, chestnut.

sound   Healthy and free from defect, especially with regard to wind and limb, at the time of examination, taking into account the use for which the pony is intended. As well as its everyday use, 'sound' has legal implications: if you buy a pony as 'sound in wind and limb' you can return it if you find it to be, say, lame from a condition that was present at the time of sale.

speedy cut   Cut on the leg arising from defective movement at fast paces.

splayfooted   With the front feet turning out: a bad conformation defect.

stable rug   Any rug intended for use in the stable only.

stall   Compartment in which a horse stands tied, like a cow being milked: a 'loosebox' is one in which he walks around free.

stallion   Uncastrated male horse or pony over three years old. Also called 'entire'.

star   White mark or patch on the forehead.

stargazing   Poking the nose and raising the head in an attempt to escape the pressure on a snaffle bit.

stocked up   With filled legs, that is, legs swollen with fluid (see page 214).

stocking   White on leg reaching to the knee.

strawberry   See roan.

surcingle   Belt going round the pony's body behind the front legs, for keeping a rug in place, for attaching side reins, breastband, chains, etc.

temperature   About 100.6°F (38°C) taken rectally.

terrets   Metal rings on driving harness through which the reins run.

tied up   Stiff behind after a hard day especially from azoturia.

tucked up   See run up.

tugs   Loops through which the shafts run on driving harness.

twitch   Stick with a loop of rope or chain attached to one end. The loop is slipped over the pony's top lip and the stick twisted until the loop tightens severely. This usually forces the pony to stand still when he otherwise would not e.g. when difficult to shoe. The use of a twitch is generally to be deplored as it frightens and hurts the pony.

underrun   With a pocket of pus under the sole of the foot, arising from a puncture wound or corns.

vice   Like the term sound, 'vice' has a specific legal meaning as well as its everyday one. A pony sold as 'free from vice' is guaranteed not to have a habit of rearing, bolting, kicking, biting or any of the stable vices, and can be returned if such a habit is found.

wall-eyed   With blue or blue and white eyes, except in the case of a blue-eyed cream. Wall-eyed ponies sometimes, though not always, have a little difficulty seeing in bright sunlight, especially after coming out of the dark.

warble   Large, noisy fly which tends to panic ponies. The eggs are laid under the pony's skin and after travelling up to the centre of the back the grubs develop under the skin there, forming a hard lump. This finally bursts, releasing the fly, but the grub can be pressed out earlier and destroyed. Warble flies have been eradicated from large areas of Britain and are no longer the problem they once were.

warm-blooded   Not an original type but rather one which has been developed through careful breeding in Holland, Germany and other north European countries: a large docile horse suitable for eventing and dressage.

weaving   Stable vice of rocking from one side to the other, but also sometimes used to mean plaiting (q.v.).

whistling   Sound made at a gallop by a horse with defective vocal cords, like roaring only less severe. An unsoundness of wind.

white   White ponies are called grey unless they are albino, i.e. with pink skin and eyes.

windgall   Soft, puffy swelling just above the fetlock at the bottom of the flexor tendon. Common in ponies that have done years of hard work e.g. hunting, windgalls do not cause lameness (any hot or painful swelling in this area is not a windgall). They can be taken down for cosmetic purposes, e.g. showing, with carefully padded tight bandages.

zebra stripes   Black stripes at the back of the knee, seen especially in dun ponies.

Index